2014 First Edition, First Printing
Williams Summit Publishers
(208) 861.1519

For additional copies of this book,
please contact Amazon.com or
the author at knealew@gmail.com.

ISBN 978-1-4991-4962-3
Vol. 2, ISBN 978-1-5030-0012-4

Design by Dominique Etcheverry, bydominique.com

Aged in Saltwater

A Journey Through the Pacific Islands

R.K. "Dick" Williams

For my Grandpa Joe Williams,
who showed me that a
well-tuned vessel requires only
light steerage at the helm.

We shall not cease from exploration.
And the end of all our exploring
Will be to arrive where we
Started
And know the place for the first time.

—T.S. Eliot

Acknowledgments

My thanks to Con Hilberry for the use of
his poems, and to my father who encouraged,
inspired, and edited long after I was ready
to give up. This book is evidence of the love
and respect in our very special relationship.

November 2014, Second Edition
R. K. "Dick" Williams

The Route of the "Blue Orpheus"

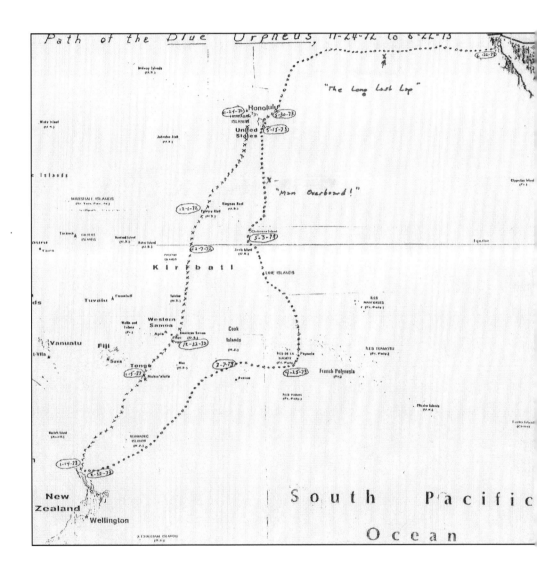

To the Reader

The ten months I spent in the South Pacific in 1972 aged me considerably, but I don't think my account of those travels will have that effect on you. For one thing, you will need only a few hours—not the better part of a year—to get to New Zealand and back via the *Blue Orpheus,* even allowing for a good many landfalls on interesting islands.

For another thing, there's quite a difference between attending and participating; for instance, attending a wedding isn't quite like getting married yourself. Or more to the point, observing a baptism doesn't have the same effect, ministers say, as getting baptized, personally. You are cordially invited to attend four "baptisms."

What happened to me in the South Pacific amounted to "immersions" in four of nature's elements. There was a shipboard baptism of fire, literally. There was a prolonged "baptism of air" in the form of a tropical hurricane. There was even more extended exposure to saltwater in its endlessly varied moods and conditions. Finally, though I'm stretching the point to call encounters with bureaucracies a "baptism of earth," I did experience a number of bureaucratic conflicts, and they definitely had an aging effect. (You will be spared most of those details, however.)

Finally, the South Pacific islands are places for youthful, innocent spirits, and I think you might even come to feel somewhat younger as a result of sharing, vicariously, a little joy with lovely, friendly people who brighten their small corners of our world.

As a youngster in a somewhat history- and literature-oriented family, I used to hear more than most kids did about the four ancient elements. Some Greeks built a philosophy of life upon them; Shakespeare and his contemporaries still believed in them. In fact, Shakespeare and company explained differences among people on the basis of "humors"— basic body "fluids" derived from earth, air, fire, and water. A "melancholy" person had too much "earth humor," a "choleric" person had too much "fire humor," and so on.

I also heard about a special fifth element, the mythical "phlogiston." It was supposed to be wonderful stuff, combining the best of the four elements and none of the worst. A symbol of ultimately high quality things and personalities. During my great traveling adventures I was never baptized in "the true phlogiston." But I'm not so sure I didn't get an occasional glimpse of something supernaturally wonderful, as for instance during that moment when a school of dolphins decided to protect the *Blue Orpheus* and her crew, and then perhaps saved our lives.

After thinking a long time about that experience and other memorable adventures, I finally decided it would be fun to share them—and I sincerely hope you enjoy the following pages.

—R.K.W.

TABLE OF CONTENTS

Part 1: Outward Bound

1. the man who wasn't there

When the nightmare begins, I am cursing helplessly, frantically, at sea on a sailboat... I've lost him. Son of a bitch, I've lost him.

A minute ago he was a hundred fifty yards out, waving an arm, hanging onto that goddam fishing ball. But I took the wrong tack for this crazy current…We lost too much time. First we dropped sails and I dove in after him, with a line around my waist. A stupid waste of precious seconds. Underestimated the strong cross currents.

Too panicked to think clearly, I took too long to put a man on the bow to do nothing but keep Randy in sight.

So now he's gone, disappeared, just like that, and it's so quiet. Christ, maybe he's still up enough to see us as we sail away. My God, until dark—another few minutes—of course he can see us, with our fifty-five foot mast.

How did this happen? What am I doing in the Pacific Ocean, hundreds of miles from land, skippering a 39' sailboat from New Zealand to Mexico, with no master's license…

How did this idiot come to be on board, anyway? From the start, he gave me nothing but trouble.

New trouble, big trouble now, as a corpse. A skipper takes responsibility for the lives of his crew, and I've just lost a life. My fault. What in the hell do I do now. Take another look—but, shit, where? Quit spotting for thirty seconds, and nobody has a clue where to even start looking. No horizon to relate a position to. Just blue water, blue sky, both darkening now with twilight. He's lost his chance by now. Gone—his life on my head. I want to die. I've tried so hard to survive, and now I want to die…

The scene disappears, consciousness returns. The pain remains. This nightmare doesn't recur as often as it used to, now that decades have gone by—but I don't understand why it comes at all. During that emergency and several other life-or-death crises we made mistakes, but after all we did save Randy's unworthy ass. The rest of us survived, too.

That incredible journey didn't just take me across physical miles of earth and sea. And a course of instruction in responsibility wasn't what I bargained for, starting the voyage—but now it looms very large and long in my recollections.

You know how time changes perspectives on everything, or covers a scene with a third eyelid? But then sometimes that eyelid lifts, unexpectedly, bringing back a spot in time as though it was just happening—and I find myself just sitting there, sails luffing, boggled all over again at my dilemma.

Years later, after a tragedy where loss of life was final and real, not just a "might have been," perhaps the early sea experience, desperate though it was, helped to preserve my sanity. Supervising a young pilot in a mountain flying charter business, I let him take over a flight that had originally been mine. The kid wanted all the flying he could get. My responsibilities included judging the way his emotional state might be affecting his professional ability. And instead of grounding him, I helped load his airplane, dispatched his flight, and went home for a beer and a shower.

Then I spent the night crawling up the mountain in the dark, working towards the remains of the fire—aluminum mixed with pine, mixed with flesh—helping pick up the remains of airplane and human bones, wondering why I gave the kid that flight, wondering what went wrong. Wondering why I hadn't sensed and acted on his impatience and anger, why I hadn't lightened the plane load, why a routine trip had ended in deaths. That nightmare was real. It taught me something new about pain.

2. the man who was there

Late in a tame summer, thanks to Tom, an exciting new possibility suddenly popped up. He phoned to ask an interesting question: "Dick, are you interested in a sail to the South Pacific?"

Dear Tom. He had a gift for making discoveries, for sharing insights, for asking mind-blowing questions—for tutoring, for livening up daily existence. My college years with him had opened new worlds. At Berkeley Tom taught me to bake bread, taught me about Bob Dylan, taught me the philosophy of cheesecake, tried to teach me to act. He

A sister ship to the "Orpheus"

knew how to remove himself from a scene, gain perspective on a situation as it happened—not later, not the fifteen years it took me. I loved him. Now, months after we had left Berkeley, Tom was still introducing me to the world.

I never guessed what would eventually put a wall between us. As things turned out, I lost him on the trip. I had other losses, but he probably mattered the most.

This time, as we talked, I learned our transportation could be a sailboat. The *Blue Orpheus*. In Honolulu, going to Auckland. First Mate injured, needed a replacement. Tom was going, as crew. The owner, DJ, was in Long Beach.

My father and I had spent the latter part of the "tame" summer together at the house, having a great time, actually. He also had been tutoring me—my private literature course, books like *Samuel Johnson* by Boswell and *Tom Jones*. We had talked about the past, our dreams, our future. He was the first one to fly with me when I got my license.

Oddly enough, Tom's question struck us both as perfectly natural, no surprise, but very exciting. Why not? So we went together to meet DJ in his small Long Beach apartment.

We got there after dark. DJ had an upstairs apartment with an outside stairway. Nothing fancy. Tom had already identified DJ as a former airline pilot, air force pilot, and pilot-navigator. An experienced sailor. But what a lot about him we didn't know then.

"Hey. Come on in. Glad you made it." An overweight man who carried it well met us. Laughing blue eyes, full of mischief. An instantly likable fellow.

"You're gonna love this boat. She raced in the Transpac last year. Did real well. We've modified the hell out of her, all set up with heavy gear, the best of everything. I can't wait to get going on this trip. It's gonna be a gas!" Dad asked him some about his experience, and he told us how he had been around boats all his life, how he was designing his own 12 meter racer to be built in Auckland. He impressed us.

"We've got a lot of work to do to get ready. I'm stuck right here for now, getting insurance and supply details done that we need to get here. With that guy getting hurt over there, I really need some help. What I'd like is for you to get over there right away with the ham radio and some other equipment, and finish installing that auxiliary engine."

He pulled out a gallon jug of Red Mountain wine, and iced our glasses to cool it. He described the islands, where we were going to stop, the good things about what to expect. And he had some great pictures.

The other five guys and I, plus one girl, got a great deal: $1,300 apiece to crew to Auckland and return to Honolulu. Same as the airfare, for a nine-month, once-in-a-lifetime experience. That was the way DJ sold it, anyway. Sounded great to me. I knew zip about Coast Guard rules, insurance, or license requirements that DJ had to deal with. (Didn't really care either. On matters of rules and regulations, I get anarchistic.)

DJ seemed a kindred spirit on that point—without specifically saying so, he conveyed the belief that most rules, trivial and meaningless, amount to nothing more than red tape meant to make someone seem important.

Our first meeting with this amazing man left us with a feeling of reality, a feeling that a great adventure lay ahead of me.

3. the Blue Orpheus and her crew

So I **flew** to Honolulu, with my gear, a ham radio, and other sailing paraphernalia. I trudged in late at night with about a hundred pounds of awkward baggage. Tom was waiting there with the rest of an impatient crew. We leaned back in the cockpit and drank beer as we inhaled the tropic air and enjoyed the gentle rocking sensation of a sailboat in the ocean. They all wondered where DJ was. Overdue to sail, DJ's sailors were pissed off.

Though several crew members demanded to know what the hell was keeping DJ, Tom's anticipation of adventures ahead made it a good reunion for me. We had left school in June, now November brought us together again. My arrival, coming directly from DJ, relaxed the crew—relieved their growing anxiety that they had put their money into some kind of sham.

We got drunk. Hawaiian weather, living on a sailboat around a hub of activity, salt spray in the air, the promise of South Sea romance, all helped to make everyone happier.

Tom looked the same. Skinny, with straight, almost stringy dirty blond hair, sharp features. You would notice and remember his deep-set, light but intense blue, eyes. He dressed like a hobo. Shirt never completely tucked in, often buttoned out of alignment, sleeves unraveled. Pants hung on him. Often a home rolled cigarette dangled between his fingers. A lot of smiles and laughs. Tom saw humor in just about everything, even his romance with Peggy Dame (he called her "Peggy Day," after the Bob Dylan number). That song and "Stuck Inside of Mobile with the Memphis Blues Again" were his favorite Dylan pieces. At least he vocalized those two a lot, though you could hardly call it singing.

Neither Tom nor I had ever sailed on the ocean—in fact I don't think Tom had even lake-sailed. But he craved the experience, like the rest of us, and wanted to explore New Zealand. Among the whole crew, only DJ had previously done blue water sailing.

I fell in with Dana, a tall, slightly goofy-looking rock climber from Michigan. Ben Franklin glasses, long beard, easygoing, nice guy. He took me climbing with him on Oahu, wanted me to rappel off a two hundred foot cliff. It terrified me. Always afraid of heights, I just couldn't oblige him.

The episode made me wonder about handling different kinds of fear—the kind that comes from ignorance, the kind that comes from panic. Once you have finally conquered a fear, respect—both self respect and respect for the thing you used to fear—can take its place.

Halfway to New Zealand Dana and I, the only crew that hadn't gotten seasick, made a bet on who would weaken first. Two days out of Auckland, in some rough squalls, Dana lost—the bet, among other things.

In the forward cabin lived Mike and Corny, our first resident couple—an overweight, under confident pair. As the cook-to-be, Corny would be taking on the worst job on a boat. I came to sympathize with anyone stuck in a small, unhandy galley, where the smell of diesel, exhaust, and bilge overpowered any food aromas. Being sick yourself, preparing meals in a stinking hole for miserable people all around you, has got to take the determination of a pit bulldog.

Looking back, I see Corny as a good cook—not a great one, but passable—and resolute. Definitely better than what followed, and definitely a better contributor than her roommate Mike, an "unnatural" sailor. We had little patience with him. He never learned to hold a course or change a sail. A true blue, eighteen-carat landlubber.

A crew member named Jack, a scuba diver like me, turned into a sailor, as I did. An engineer on leave from his job in the Bay area, single and set in his ways, older than the rest of us, Jack came across as always a little edgy, impatient, somewhat militaristic, wanting immediate results. We couldn't match his physical shape. No problems with him, at first anyway, but he and I never got close.

DJ—when he did eventually show up—proved as likable a man as we had ever encountered. DJ and I became good friends. His great stories, his absolutely charming style brought him women, boats, crews, equipment, and who knows what else. He made you feel like his best friend, and that feeling made you eager to do anything for him.

Before long, once we were sailing, he began talking to me on a very personal, man to man level. I loved it. I'd never had a relationship like it. Recently I had been getting closer to my father, but not as a fellow adventurer, a buddy and partner. DJ was forty-three, I was twenty-two. He had traveled around the world in the military, worked as a professional pilot, sailed all over, had seen the world from a perspective I never imagined. What I had seen were schoolbooks.

DJ was rarely serious. He laughed a lot, especially around women. Being about thirty pounds overweight he didn't exactly look like a playboy—but he sure achieved like one. A charmer, the most devastating I've seen, to this day. And even after all that eventually happened, I smile when I think of him. (I doubt that anyone else who had much to do with the *Blue Orpheus* could make that claim.)

What a name—*Blue Orpheus*—an ironic self prophecy. In Greek mythology, the musician *Orpheus* went down to hell to bring back his departed wife, but, because of temptation and inability to follow orders, blew his mission. Before *Orpheus* had led his wife all the way out of hell, he took a forbidden peek, and lost her forever.

When DJ and his confused friends named the boat, they hit on a name they thought meant "orifice," or "making a hole in the ocean," or something weird like that. Anyway, the boat and its crews lived under that mistake from the start, all the way to the vessel's final demise.

Soon after meeting Tom and the crew in Honolulu, I learned that the first mate I replaced had taken off with three

Tom and Dana work on loading the boat

sets of Barlow winches, muttering about being ripped off by DJ. He had injured his back while hauling the transmission out for repair.

The boat immediately fascinated me with its air of something foreign, sleek, and sophisticated. (That view changed with familiarity.) DJ had modified an Ericson 39 for racing and heavy weather (thank God). She had several tons of lead in the keel, an enlarged rudder, wheel steering, a 55' aluminum mast with internal halyards, oversized 5/8" rigging, a diesel auxiliary, and a food freezer. Having no self-steering mechanism, the *Blue Orpheus* eventually performed what might be one of the longest hand-helmed sails in recent history—11,000 nautical miles.

We carried an emergency life raft that, unfortunately, we never tested. I regret that neglect. The rest of the equipment became so questionable that we naturally suspected the raft. By the end of the trip, anyway, we would have liked to know whether the thing worked.

We had an excellent navigational library, three sextants, including a German Plath with a zero index error, and an Air Force bubble sextant. We carried a ham radio and a ship-to-shore, and a lot of spare rigging and engine parts. The fiberglass hull felt cold and impersonal, especially towards the end, but it stayed in one piece. It was just about the only thing that did.

We stayed in Waikiki almost three weeks. On this visit to Hawaii, my third, for the first time I didn't feel like a tourist. On my first trip I had just graduated from high school and was traveling with a friend, on a budget so tight we slept on the beach and hauled our suitcases with us twenty-four hours a day.

4. getting the drift

Before DJ got there, I did a lot of diving, helping a commercial diver catch tropical fish and collect coral. That culminated in a memorable night dive for lobster. All divers survived, though for a time the issue remained in serious doubt.

The divers' "mother boat" held seven of us: three professional diving instructors, two commercial divers, a new diver, and me. Eight passengers, actually: Rick had a little dog that constantly accompanied us and stood watch in the little twin outboard when we dove for coral.

My three-man dive team included an instructor and the new man. When the beginner got low on air, we three surfaced. The faint sound of barking told us we had drifted about three hundred yards from the boat, much further than we had planned. The new guy had an air vest and snorkeled back to the boat. The instructor and I went back hunting, continuing my first unforgettable night dive. On a spacewalk, weightless in a dark, foreign, fantastic place, an astronaut must have something in common with a nighttime scuba diver. If daytime diving takes you into another world, night diving offers another universe.

The lobster and moray eels, which co-habitate holes in the coral, come out at night to feed. The eels' heads, awesomely large when poking out from their holes, almost seem to fit their huge, ugly worm-like bodies as they swim, exposed. The lobster sedately walk across the sandy bottom, feeding—until you sneak up and grab one. Then an explosion of sand, fins, claws, and air bubbles shocks and scares you. A lobster's strength also surprises you as you battle to hang on and wrestle your catch into the bag.

After we caught one, we surfaced because of my low air supply. Shouts were coming from the boat and all around us. The lights of Waikiki looked dim—Diamond Head, shark territory, too close—and the boat much too far off.

We both had air vests, and began surface swimming towards the boat. We didn't get much closer, but were tiring fast. The shouts continued.

A familiar feeling began: elevated heart rate, increased, shallow breathing, a strange dry, cottony taste permeating the mouth—panic. We and the other divers faced a life-threatening situation. It called for a quick re-grouping of the mind.

Stop those physical symptoms, take some deep breaths, try to relax, and organize a plan. In spite of chaos around us, we had to ignore the noise and distraction, and just get back to that boat. Closer than the others, we gutted it out, swimming as hard as we could, and reached the boat. Maybe the current had started to weaken. I know we had. Near exhaustion as the guy in the boat helped pull us in, we couldn't even understand his excited babble.

We didn't need to, though. We knew what had happened. The boat hadn't drifted; we had tied its anchor line to coral on the bottom. A powerful current had caught all of us, separated us from each other. Only we three had made it back to the boat.

Currents still gripped the other divers, who were hollering at us in the darkness. The poor kid in the boat by himself couldn't do anything. He didn't have enough air to go below and untie the anchor, and he couldn't get the engines started either.

My diving buddy got one engine going while I went below again to untie the anchor. By the time we had our boat under way, another vessel had answered the distress calls and picked up two divers.

We got the others, nearly exhausted by then, who hadn't been wearing air vests—an almost fatal error. They had dropped their tanks and weights to lighten up.

We went back to the harbor without saying a word. An hour later, wined and lobstered, we loosened up some. But not much. When you've been that scared, even fresh lobster doesn't quite settle your nerves.

Two "liquids," air and water, give you nothing to hang on to. After experiencing the scariness of "immersion" in them—flying and sailing/swimming—I've sometimes wanted to leave them and never return. But they can possess a person. The sky and the sea can generate a special kind of addictive respect, born out of fear and other quite different feelings: awe, wonder—and, probably, love.

The fear never really disappears, you never really beat it. You lose track of a lot of things, but not certain moments of panic. They serve as reminders, they teach respect. Long after that night diving episode I learned that years later it could be even be scarier than it was at the time. You live with it—you live with the fear, your respect continues to grow, as does your determination to become less careless.

After thousands of hours of flying and many months of sailing, I'm probably as comfortable in air and water as most anybody. And I strongly prefer surviving in them. I don't want them to beat me. In due time, earth and fire can have what's left of me.

They say the water off Waikiki is polluted now. What a crime. It was very nice water then. Cousteau said something like "our salvation is with the ocean, and destroying it, we destroy ourselves."

5. the wizard

Even I had started to wonder about DJ by the time he finally appeared. But then he immediately took perfect control. He fended off angry questions, made friends with everyone, told a few great sea stories, and set a departure date one week away. The self-confidence, the convincing answers, the masterful directions, made us all relax. Our skipper was in command.

He brought a couple of stewardess friends over to the boat for cocktails one evening. We could hardly believe what we saw. I had never before encountered anyone so self-assured, easy going, natural, almost innocent-appearing. Like he didn't really care. He had a great laugh, more like a giggle, actually. You could tell the women loved it. The man both intrigued me and roused my envy. He seemed to have a great life, knew what he had, and enjoyed every moment of it.

But were we a ship of fools, blindly heading into the storm season? A trimaran that had sailed south limped back six days later with its hull broken by the high seas. We rationalized: what else would you expect of junky trimarans, anyway? The Coast Guard had paid us a visit before DJ arrived, asking questions about our plans. Were we charter? We didn't know. DJ, though, convinced us of his solid legal standing. The Coast Guard had no jurisdiction in international waters, but anyway he had provided standard arrangements—a great deal for us, the crew.

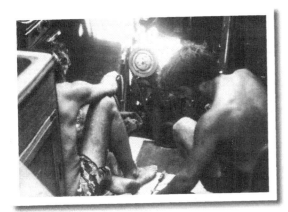

Ready work began in earnest. Tom and I teamed up as The Bilge Rats. We emptied all the hatches to check, inventory, and re-stash equipment. The auxiliary diesel, replacing a smaller gasoline engine, still needed a lot of frustrating attention in a compartment too small for it. (Changing an oil filter took four hours and skinned knuckles.) We rebuilt the broken steering system. To check chafe points and halyard wear, I climbed the mast in the boatswain's chair—a job not much easier than trying

Working on the diesel meant dirty bilge water and skinned knuckles

to rappel off a high cliff with Dana. But I had more desire to succeed at the mast.

We all learned to tie a bowline. Nobody in the whole crew had even known how, for Christ's sake! We practiced them with our eyes closed, lying on our sides, upside down, hanging on the stanchions—every possible contorted position. (The practice came in handy. I tied a lot of bowlines at night during squalls.) We heard "man overboard" lectures which proved practical, and prophetic.

During this preparation interval DJ began working on me as "his man." He gave me special time and instruction, made me teacher's pet. I loved it, reveled in it too happily to recognize the jealousy it was breeding, even before our launch.

6. Palmyra

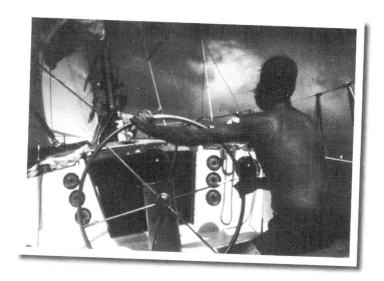

**The first few days at sea, you always have
to get adjusted. Even when we frequently sailed
in and out of port, finding our sea legs would
take a day or so. But this shakedown leg was
different, unexpectedly complex.**

Changing worlds, from land to sea, required a whole
new set of habits. We didn't know each other. We couldn't
guess how the boat would act, once it had reached its own
element. We didn't know what to expect about much of
anything. Before routines had really established themselves,
even before we all had sea legs, everyone except Dana and me

Our first taste of weather arrived in the night as a line of squalls

had learned from experience which side of the boat to be on when you're seasick.

On that first sail, also, DJ and I soon cemented our friendship. He began teaching me navigation and details about sailing the boat.

DJ always seemed to choose approaching nightfall as the time to leave land. He could have had several reasons, including convenience in avoiding red tape. But he had psychological grounds, too. When you think you've left a place, but still see it eight hours later, you get demoralized, especially in rough weather. A crew also finds it easier to get into the routine at night.

On our first leg to Palmyra, we had nice, easy sailing. Actually, we stayed pretty much trouble free all the way down to Auckland. I've wondered why the fates decided to save up the difficult times, and give them all to me, with no DJ around to lead us out of trouble.

I worked hard on navigation. For the first time in my life, I got fascinated with something mathematical. In my high school days, only a teacher's charity—and probably his desire to keep me out of a repeat class—kept me from flunking Algebra I. What's more, I hadn't cared. The concepts of higher math could go their way, I would go mine. During my final university years, I hadn't concerned myself much about time, either. The hip Berkeley anti-time attitude grew out of a rejection of an artificially fast American pace—a refusal to live by time schedules that diminished consciousness of cosmic time and space!

The funny thing about navigation was, it brought time back to cosmic movement, universal meaning. So I could accept timepieces, if only extremely accurate ones. I slowly understood that each second had precise meaning and relation to the movement and placement of every star and planet. Knowing those celestial moves could tell me my own location on earth, in sync with the stars. A tremendous revelation for me. The drugged out freaks of Berkeley could look at the stars and say, "Hey, wow, man!" but so could I, with their wonder plus some understanding of and appreciation for real and giant events.

I spent my spare time keeping a journal, writing letters, working with DJ, and reading nautical reference books. The crew took two hour watches, with eight hours off. The navigator didn't have to work the helm. His job was "easier"—merely to get us to an island nine hundred miles south of Hawaii, four by six miles small, with the highest point a ninety foot cocoanut (sic) palm tree:

Palmyra, an atoll discovered by the ship Palmyra in 1802. Uninhabited. At the western end of the atoll, a sunken reef contains many small coral patches and heads, either completely or nearly awash, through which it is almost impossible...to navigate...

Dangerous tide rips have been reported...A stranded wreck, conspicuous from seaward...may be used as an aid in approaching...Another stranded wreck is located about 650 yards northwestward...Entrance should not be attempted unless the weather is clear, sun shining, tide at flood and the wind is less than 10 knot...

Rainfall is heavy and humidity high. The average annual rainfall is 100 to 180 inches. Rain occurs almost daily. Heavy rain squalls come up suddenly from the southwest...Strong and variable currents may be expected...

An explosives dumping area is established westward of Palmyra. [Sailing Directions, H.O. 80, Sec. 12-36.]

* * *

Fish caught at Palmyra Island are said to be poisonous; violent fish poisoning has occurred, some with fatal consequences…[Sailing Directions, H.O. 80, Sec. 12-36.]

On our way to the island, and before we reached it, we caught our first tuna, a wonderful fish, different from what you find in cans. Better than trout. We trolled with a long heavy line with a rubber shock cord at the boat end, using a variety of hooks and lures.

On the entire trip down we never went long without fresh tuna or Mai Mai, Hawaiian "dolphin." The Mai Mai (neither mammals, nor related to the dolphin), die a gruesome, awesome death. The natives say they change colors thirty-one times from the moment they leave the water until they die. Speckles change to rainbows to stripes to dots before your eyes. Every hue of the prism. The process makes one wonder what else goes on inside.

Occasionally we would drop sail and jump overboard, in glassy water. Swimming in the open ocean can cause mind games—and deterioration. I never felt smaller than I did below the surface of that clear blue water, knowing it went a mile or two straight down, four hundred miles sideways to a beach. I couldn't let myself get very far from the boat, "Mother" *Orpheus*, who provided food, sustenance, shelter, safety, mobility, life itself—to me, her embryo, a creature totally helpless without her. No wonder ships take on a feminine gender. No wonder I got so attached to her and will never forget her.

We witnessed the magic of porpoises, beginning with some merely friendly first encounters. These cheerful friends seemed drawn to our night music; up to fifty would appear occasionally to play with the boat, jumping in front of the bow and racing alongside. They gave all of us a sense of wonder. We couldn't help imagining that these ocean mammals were trying to communicate, maybe tell us something we desperately needed to know. As our record will eventually show, on the way home we had strong evidence of that kind of concern for human life.

A line of squalls, our first taste of weather, arrived during a pitch black, moonless night, as we approached Palmyra. The wind would make 360-degree shifts, and the helmsman had to read the wind instead of the compass. Tom came on watch about midnight and got confused steering through one squall. The wheel got away from him, spun, and jammed tight at the end of its travel. DJ and I crawled down the starboard hatch, and in contorted positions (standard posture down there), working through openings about three by two feet), with flashlight, hammer, and chisel, we finally freed the tiller.

Tom felt incapable and foolish. He shouldn't have. You can't really fault people for unforeseen problems during their first experience with squalls—pretty strong ones. We were all learning.

* * *

Landfall. 05° 52' N, 162° 06' W. The 960-nautical-mile leg had taken us eight days. Our book of Sailing Directions told us what to expect:

> *Abundant sea and migratory birds and a few turtles are found [near Palmyra, which]…has unfavorable weather, and is the only island in its latitude where fresh westerlies occur. A tropical front hovers in the vicinity of the island caused by the meeting of the northeast and southeast trades…northeast trades prevail, with an average velocity of 10 to 12 knots. There are frequent squalls of short duration and occasional winds up to 22 knots, but typhoons are very infrequent…*
>
> *A 400 foot ship's pier and a boat pier are located in West Lagoon. The ship's pier was reported in poor condition in 1964…There is an airfield. [Sailing Directions, H.O. 80, Sec. 12-36.]*

This first passage, from Honolulu to Palmyra, showed us the adventure of sailing, enthralled us. Except for one bad night we had good weather, and those moderately unpleasant few hours only enhanced the excitement, the feeling of high romance.

I suspect DJ made a navigational error, although he never said and I never asked. An excellent navigator, he hadn't practiced for over a year. The day after the squalls, he did a lot of intense plotting, then changed tack and course. About three p.m. Tom sighted land. We approached from the east, along the south side, and into the lagoon at the southwest corner.

You don't forget the experience of your First Landfall, your first witnessing that celestial navigation has actually brought you safely to land. Those lines of position and declination angles and crazy looking plotting charts served a real purpose. You go up on deck, see water and sky—then also birds, surf, land, and trees. Theory and fact connect.

You never forget what your nose tells you, either. The smells of land. I noticed, even with a notoriously terrible sniffer. You get a crazy mix of everything not sea or bilge—everything that goes with normal everyday living on earth. Until you have left the earth for days and returned, you can't quite imagine the encounter.

Sometimes you smell land even before you see it. It gets in the wind and travels out to you, with the birds. Maybe in the water too, with coconuts and palm leaves. In all my life, no aromas ever impressed me as much as those first sniffs of land after eight days at sea.

You have been moving along powered by two basic elements, wind and sea, the way old timers traveled. Now, as the boat comes onto land, the noise of the hull against the water somehow sounds louder and closer.

You suddenly appreciate the beauty of the land—the third element, earth. White sand, swaying coconut palms, green vegetation to offset the thousands of miles of blue water, and blue sky. And the blue water finally meeting land with tremendous white breakers.

Throughout the scene you couldn't find much external evidence of fire, that "fourth element," but of course it lurked there, mostly hidden. Heraclitus said fire will discern and catch with all things—a strange, true remark, warning that fire gets some things fast, and some things slow (like oxidation), but nothing escapes. When you think you are seeing only earth, air, and water, you are in fact seeing the effects of fire as well. When this transforming element gets out of control, you've got trouble—a kind I mistakenly failed to anticipate. So anyway, on this first landfall, only the miraculous fifth element phlogiston seemed to be missing, but I wasn't totally convinced it wasn't there, too.

I took the helm while DJ piloted from the bow with our harbor chart in hand. We all tried to spot reefs blocking the narrow entrance. Once on solid ground, we couldn't walk straight. The white sand beaches turned into moving masses of land and hermit crabs. We felt a little like them— awkward, eager to savor the land, and have the sea keep its distance for the time being.

"CRABS AT LOW TIDE"
Pry invisible bits of green
off the rocks and lift them,
Delicately, to the moving flame
Of their mouths. They nibble grain,
These sea-sparrows,
their song the thin click of claws.

The ocean keeps its distance. Then a fuse
Burns white, right to left across
The water; the beach smokes and roars
Breaking the big news

Even on this distant county.
After the spume, the rocks are empty.

Out of a crack, a red leg tries the silence-
Then scores of legs. The crabs are back.
Everyone samples the lettuce, and the rock
Honors the reticence
Of shells that bow sideways and do not speak.
It honors the courtly elbows of a dance.

—Conrad Hilberry

Except for a road grader and fork lift, the old military equipment had gone bad. The jungle was reclaiming the airstrips. Because of oil and bilge garbage from war days, you couldn't see any deeper than twenty feet or so into the water of the shark-infested lagoon. What a mess.

Still, we liked being on land, living for a while on a flat, still boat. We gloated over finding a fresh water shower rigged to a large overhead tank. After long, plentiful showers the crew could shave, have haircuts, and preen in front of a large mirror. A clothesline rigged from boat supplies made the laundromat complete. We dined ashore, around a fire. DJ had ruled, no booze on the boat, but on land a few bottles of wine and brandy appeared. Tom and I sat by the fire late at night with our secret bottle of brandy, feeling a long way from our Berkeley house and the campus scene, but still close. The teacher-student roles were changing, though, and that made a difference. I was learning from DJ now, not from Tom. Though I had never surpassed Tom in anything, that pattern might change soon. Tom was responding to the situation, I thought, by growing more competitive.

Several years after our visit a murder took place on Palmyra. A couple arrived in a leaky cruddy vessel with hardly any supplies or equipment. They found another boat tied up at the pier, owned by an older couple enjoying a retirement cruise. The younger pair murdered the older couple, stole their boat, and eventually headed back for Hawaii. When friends of the victims recognized the boat they launched an investigation. No one ever found the bodies, but the girl eventually told the story, blaming her boyfriend. I visualize the harbor and old pier vividly, but can hardly imagine murder in that peaceful setting.

Before leaving Palmyra, we cleaned the boat bottom and I taught Tom some scuba basics. We worked some more on the steering system, tightened the drive shaft on the engine, and changed the oil and filter. If I ever have my own boat, I'll be able to walk around the damned engine. I truly hated working on that misplaced, misbegotten bastard which had no tolerance for hands or wrenches.

7. navigation

Navigation.
Dick Williams, temporary navigator.

My mission (should I care to accept it) was to get the *Orpheus* to Tutuila, American Samoa, about 1,300 miles from Palmyra, an island on the other side of the equator, and at least twelve days' sailing.

Just to build my confidence, shortly after leaving Palmyra we couldn't start the (damned) engine, which we normally ran a couple of hours a day to keep the food freezer cold and to charge two big marine batteries. Even with this dual battery system, we couldn't get it going. Finally we

An ideal evening at sea

found a short in the bottom bilge pump wiring, and solved the problem. By pure luck, we had enough juice left to start up and get re-charged.

Heavier weather hit us, one squall up to thirty-five knot gusts and about force 6 (22–27 knots on the Beaufort Scale). Taking turns at the helm, almost everyone managed—more or less—fearlessly.

Doldrums in between squalls. Jack fixed the wiring of the wind instruments. We enjoyed some swims, but I spent most of my time at the plotting charts, which got pretty sweat soaked. We had plenty of hot weather, which I've never handled well. Also, though I don't like to figure out puzzling subjects by myself, I didn't want to ask DJ too many questions. So I spent a lot of time "pouring" over the books (dripping sweat on them).

In school B's and C's had come to me without much effort. I've already admitted sloughing on the tough subjects, winging it, getting by on bullshit and luck. Navigation became one of the first hard subjects I didn't just settle for less on. So if I could manage this second leg and hit that Samoan island right on target, my pride would take great comfort.

I spent a lot of time on the writings of Nathaniel Bowditch (1773–1838), an English sailor, astronomer, mathematician, and world-class navigator who produced volumes on navigation that every serious sailor owns and understands. Bowditch doesn't just start you out with a lot of calculations and drills—he gives you a feeling for all the navigators of history, even those before Columbus.

He admired the Polynesians who, traveling long distances without compass or sextant, must have refined navigation to a highly advanced art. Their instinct and perception must have resembled those of the birds and fish.

I learned that by the fifteenth century, astronomers had determined the sun's declination (distance from the geographic equator), for each day of the year, and put it on tables and maps. The sun's declination ranges 47 degrees, 23.5 on each side of the equator, forming the tropics of Cancer and Capricorn. The summer solstice (longest day of the year in the north) is June 21; the winter solstice, the Tropic of Capricorn, falls at the same latitude south, December 22.

At solstices the sun's zenith reaches 89°, 59' at one or the other Tropic latitude. On the equinoxes, September 23 and March 22, the sun rises at the South Pole and sets at the North Pole, reaching its zenith on the equator. At that point days and nights are the same length all over the world. Other days, the sun reaches maximum zenith at some latitude between the Tropics. (I experienced, just once, the fun of catching it at maximum. You swing the sextant around 360 degrees and the sun remains on the horizon.)

Celestial navigation begins with a three-dimensional triangle drawn from the elevated pole of the earth, a celestial body, and the zenith of the observer. The polar distance of the body (co-declination, from the almanac), its zenith distance (co-altitude, from the sextant), and the polar distance of the zenith (co-latitude of the observer) form the sides of the triangle. Next you compute the meridian angle, and comparing it with the GHA in the almanac gives you your longitude.

You have to make use of time in the navigator's sense of the word. Bowditch gives a true, terse, beautiful definition: *Time is the measure of the phase of the earth's rotation.*

In that sense, time refers to positions of celestial bodies relative to the meridians on the earth, turning fifteen degrees westward every hour. Navigation requires comparing local time with that of a reference meridian.

Bowditch reveals interesting distorting factors. For instance, 2,000 years ago the Vernal Equinox, March 22, used to go by the name, The First Point of Aries because, two millenniums ago, the sun would enter the constellation Aries in late March. But in the last 2,000 years the earth's tilt has moved the equinoxes westward thirty degrees, the equivalent of one constellation. A navigator who uses Aries as the reference meridian calls it the sidereal hour angle. However, modern navigation usually relies instead on the GHA, the Greenwich meridian angle. Nearly all books of observations and the nautical almanac pre-compute position comparisons with the GHA; the navigator merely figures from that reference. (Slightly easier than calculating sines and cosines the way Captain Cook did it.)

(For other examples of time and vision distortion— gravitational attraction produced by the moon, a satellite of earth, causes tidal motion. The resultant tidal friction lengthens earth's days by .001 per century. At night, when you think you are seeing "millions" of stars—really, suns— your naked eyes actually witness about 2,500. Those celestial bodies rise four minutes earlier each night, and appear to shift one degree west each night.)

Bowditch doesn't neglect the navigator's job of Dead Reckoning, which requires calculations based on time, speed, and distance. It got its name from Deduced Reckoning, using the Dutchman's Log. You threw an object into the sea and assumed it to be dead in the water. You figured speed in comparison to it, allowing for current and wind. Eventually Deduced Reckoning got lopped down to ded reckoning.

It surprised me to be getting interested in not only the ritual of navigation, but the theory behind those actions. The foreign, fascinating procedure began with the sextant sight, accurately timed. Then, one at a time, you follow the steps on the form, reducing the sight to a line of position (LOP), drawing the LOP on a plotting chart, interpreting it in relation to other LOPs and dead reckoning (DR).

We normally would take a morning shot at nine or ten o'clock. Then a good noon shot at the sun's highest point in the sky for that day would tell us the ship's exact latitude. After we took the third sight in late afternoon, and plotted the three sights together as a triangle, we could calculate "LOP" (line of position) and longitude. Estimating speed and distance from the morning sight would give an accurate point in the triangle on the LOP plotted from the last sight.

Then you would make allowances for other factors. Throw in boat motion, tough working conditions, DR estimates for drift, current, steering and compass deviation, lack of a taffrail log, sextant errors caused by dropping or mishandling, inaccurate time, cloud cover, and whatever other variables might exist.

As I navigated, Tom often watched me as I had watched DJ on the first leg. Though I had pretty good sextant shots—the main concern—I also made several math errors, which Tom caught, and tried to keep me from really screwing up.

I began to see navigation through Bowditch's eyes, as both a science and an art, and became immersed in both aspects. Though we think of navigation as a science, Bowditch said, it began six to eight thousand years ago as an art, and a

few practitioners still work to keep its art forms alive, especially sextants and their handling.

A few years after my encounters with Bowditch, I discovered the writing of Beryl Markham, a great pilot with a lot of respect for sailors. She also denied that science could capture all the elements and spirit of her profession; what science couldn't capture went even beyond art:

After this era of great pilots is gone, as the era of great sea captains has gone, each nudged aside by the march of inventive genius…it will be found, I think, that all the science of flying has been captured in the breadth of an instrument board, but not the religion of it.

The *Blue Orpheus*, thirty-nine by eleven feet outside, contained an inside cabin considerably smaller than that. Only the forward bunk (Mike's and Corny's) and the head afforded any privacy. The rest of us bunked two on each side, upper and lower, and the quarter bunk across from the galley (DJ's). Though seven persons overcrowded the area, DJ went for dollars instead of space. Eventually we had crews of four and five—much more comfortable. But the real problem of compatibility goes beyond spatial arrangements. What happened to Tom and me showed that even living with someone for a long time on land doesn't guarantee good relations at sea. I became convinced that only a shakedown

Tom and me in the galley

cruise—never feasible for us—could predict the "sea chemistry" of a new crew.

I found that, in good weather, the foredeck gave the best escape. Tom and I sometimes visited there, but mostly DJ and I made use of the spot, leaning against the mast together. I didn't see anyone else using it that way.

DJ began applying some devastating psychological devices. In our "mast talks," with contagious enthusiasm he revealed plans and dreams, and confided that he wanted me to share them:

"Hey, Dick, I've got some serious stuff to talk to you about. I've been watching you pretty close since we started on this thing, and you're the guy I've been looking for. I've got some great plans that you are going to love." Flattery, but music to my ears.

"Oh, yeah, what have you got going?"

"Look, the reason I'm going to New Zealand is to design and build a twelve meter racing boat. New Zealand has the best designers and builders in the world. I'm going to stay down there for awhile to work with these guys. I need someone to take over and bring the *Orpheus* back to the mainland. And that's only part of it. I own another boat, Dick, a seventy foot sloop called the *Nam Sang*. It's in L.A. and I'm going to charter it back to New Zealand. If things work out, you can captain that boat.

"You'll love it—a beautiful old boat, all re-rigged. You'll have your own stern cabin, take a girlfriend if you want." DJ's words took a while to sink in, and then I made some feeble protests.

"Jesus, DJ, I don't have the experience to do all that."

"Hey, no problem. I've been watching you. I know you

can do it. There's nothing to sailing a boat like that. Of course you'll have to get your Sailing Master's license, but that's no big deal.

"There won't be a lot of bucks at first, but I'll pay you what I can, and believe me you'll have the time of your life!"

He went on to describe life at sea—all the good, some of the bad, just enough to ignite my own dreams of freedom and responsibility. What a tremendous break to meet this guy! DJ knew just what to say, just how much, how to mix responsibility with fun. He kept me excited about the future, near and far at the same time.

Halfway through the second leg of our sail, the crew had gotten into the routine. Some of them found it boring. Sea life doesn't fit everyone. The romance doesn't last, the salt gets old. But my sea world stayed fresh and interesting. I found time to write, read, sleep, talk, think, and learn—mostly in my bunk, my nest. On the way to New Zealand I occupied the starboard lower, a good bunk because our prevailing port tack tucked me against the hull. I didn't have to use a bunk bra, a canvas sling that prevents the bunk's "contents" from spilling into the aisle.

Any engine problem made us painfully aware of crowded space. Fixing a leaky exhaust elbow, "going below," consisted of lifting the seats in the cockpit and crawling through the small hatch opening, after pulling out assorted sails, spare engine and boat parts, a Honda 50 mini-bike with folding handlebars—to name a few items—and wrestling around the steering mechanism, batteries, transmission, and drive line. (I've already expressed my feelings about an oversized motor whose routine maintenance required contortions, toleration of strong diesel bilge odors, resistance to claustrophobia, and blood sacrifices.)

Luckily, we had calm seas when the starter bendix spring began sticking—we had to continually tap the end of the starter to re-set it.

December 7, 1972. 0° 50' S, 164° 40' W (or so we recorded!). We celebrated crossing the equator at about seven a.m. (They say water drains counter-clockwise now, but that is not true.) We "virgins" making our first crossing (everyone except DJ) had to hear a few crude jokes and stories, then those dwindled down to a few hurrahs and toasts. The old traditions seem to range anywhere from taking a swim (baptism) to equatorial sexual conquests.

The porpoises that hung out with us offered special, hypnotizing entertainment. Then Mike caught a huge albacore tuna, four feet long, 115 pounds. It stopped the boat and we had to use the engine to work the monster in—the delicious monster!

Two days later, the condenser in the refrigeration and freezer system developed a saltwater leak that destroyed the whole unit. We still had a couple hundred pounds of frozen beef and pork, not to mention all the tuna. We ate like pigs and tried—ineffectively—to dry some surplus meat. Thereafter the menu took a definite turn for the worse.

Next the engine actually quit. I spent a day and a half neglecting navigation, helping Tom and DJ try to cope with it. A leaky fuel filter had pumped twenty-three gallons of diesel into the bilges and let air into the injection system. From that time on we regularly had fuel/air leaks, and never really solved the problem. We would periodically try to bleed the whole fuel system—a practical impossibility. You had to lie on your belly and scrape your knuckles to get back to all the various bleeding nipples and purge the system. A normally thirty minute job always took several hours.

Leaving the navigation chart to help on the engine was my second mistake in a row. First, in haste before going to the engine area, I had made a math error. It fouled up my navigation, and took six sweaty hours to find. Screwed up, unsure of our position, I could see DJ watching carefully— from a distance. Once he even asked how I was doing, but I had resolved to do the job myself. Just as DJ had completed his leg without my curious eyes and questions, Tom left me alone to bring us in. He probably felt an unspoken fear of messing up another guy's figures, or causing even more problems.

When sailors are expecting to see land, and it doesn't show up, you would hardly believe the way tension mounts. We had been averaging about 120 miles every noon to noon. On December 14, I recorded our position as 13° 05' S, 169° 50' W.

After getting at least two dozen requests, I announced land's assumed bearing and distance. Everyone sneakily began looking. When the island didn't appear in a few minutes, the unspoken doubts and questions became deafening. You can tell what your shipmates are thinking when they quit looking ahead, and start peeking off both beams. And you do a little of that yourself. Probably, when DJ was getting us to Palmyra and had some problems with the navigation figures, even he had his similar doubts—but he gave a great show of confidence. Later, in his position, I understood how he must have felt.

Early the next morning, before daylight, DJ found Mike steering thirty degrees off course, with no land in sight. Just before dark, the evening before, Tom had reported seeing land, and I had relished the relief and elation of my first success as navigator. When I heard what Mike had done I wanted to use him for a sea anchor. My temporary navigational triumph had disappeared along with the island.

After figuring a correction, though, we changed course; and by daybreak, off the bow, land appeared again. We docked just before noon on the fifteenth. Our 1,300-mile leg had kept us at sea twelve days.

Mission accomplished.

—Dick Williams, apprentice navigator

Mike caught a huge albacore tuna, four feet long, one hundred fifteen pounds

8. people

In contrast to Palmyra, a coral atoll, Tutuila
looms up as a lush green volcanic mountain,
beautiful to approach. Three peaks make
the island much more visible to sailors
than an atoll—Mount Pioa, with 1,717 feet
elevation; Alava, 1,609 feet high; and
Matafao, 2,141 feet. From miles out we could
see surf breaking on the northern cliffs.

Seeing people, the first in almost a month, going about their business, actually shocked us. What an unfamiliar sight! We planned to mingle with them—but as things turned out, some of us got into Tutuila society faster and deeper than we ever could have predicted.

The *Blue Orpheus* coasted into a deep, protected harbor; a big boat harbor, in fact. That first evening a luxury liner docked. After getting to know a couple of the crew, Tom and Jack pulled a bit of a sneak, with the insiders' help, and managed a free dinner and movie on board. They took considerable pride in their exploit, and the rest of us got properly envious. Food, entertainment, luxury liner style—and at such a reasonable price! But we also had some "sour grapes" thoughts about the people who try to experience the South Pacific from lounge chairs on a cruiser sundeck. We easily talked ourselves into feeling smug about doing things the tough, adventurous way.

The sailing directions provide a lot of useful information about American Samoa.

> *Its population (about 21,000 at the time of our visit) is mostly of the true Polynesian type…The climate on the islands is mild, equable, and healthy… pleasant, even at sea level…[In Pago Pago harbor] an aerial tramway spans the harbor in a north to south direction…the cable has a clearance of 152 feet…Whale Rock, of coral formation, lies in the middle of the channel inside the harbor entrance… Pago Pago, on the northwestern side of the harbor, is the largest village on the island and is the seat of the Government…*
>
> *Supplies of fresh provisions and fruits are available. Tinned foods can be purchased in large quantities. Meat is scarce, but pork and poultry are obtainable in small amounts. Ice may be obtained. Water, which has been filtered and chlorinated, is piped to the principal berths. It is available in unlimited quantities, except during the dry season which lasts about three months beginning June 15. Fuel oil, diesel oil, and gasoline are available…the hospital at Utelei is one of the best equipped…in the South Pacific Islands.*

Once ashore, we would have walked miles to find cold beer and ice cream. We soon spotted promising-looking places. The Whiskey A-Go-Go obviously offered a lot of action, and so did the Goat Island Club, the Island Moon, and the Seaside—all "Casablanca" bars, dark, smoky, old, with juke box music instead of "Sam" at the piano. The Samoan bars also had a higher noise level, plus dancing, lots of talk, lots of laughter.

The "good old days" do change with time. To someone who visited Samoa in the fifties, much less last century, the place would seem spoiled by the time we landed there (early seventies). And if we returned in the nineties, many things we enjoyed in our first exposure to the island would be gone. Today's yachting magazines indicate a sharp rise of island traffic in the last fifteen years, and it depresses a person to think of the losses that balance out those gains.

Anyway, in 1972, when Papaya, the old barmaid at the Island Moon, realized that all of us conspicuous oddballs came from "the" sailboat, she gave us friendly attention. Then she began to specialize. She bought me extra drinks and got upset when I tried to give one away. She had me all but branded as private property; she would slip away from other customers and haul me out to the dance floor. A sailor's paradise—if he happens to like aggressive partners.

Another girl (a little younger and less experienced-looking than Papaya) asked me to dance, and got both of us into trouble. Papaya ran over, only half-playfully kicked her "friend," grabbed me, and as we danced, bumped her butt against the other girl's. As the *Orpheus* crew caught one another's eyes, smirking, we could imagine ourselves to be sailors from the Bounty of a bygone century, finding warm, friendly, tropical women ready to serve and even adulate us white men.

The next morning I not only couldn't find the Bounty—I couldn't even find the *Orpheus*! My sailboat "mother" had abandoned me—holy shit! Dumbfounded, I stumbled around the dock, scratching my head, wondering what to do. After more than an hour I finally located my crew at the customs dock. The *Orpheus* had dragged anchor in the night and the crew had moved her.

9. the bridegroom Goeth

Dana, Tom, Jack, and I took the tram over
the harbor to the head of the jungle trail
heading back down to Vatia, an isolated
village accessible only by foot or boat. The
top of the tram offered a beautiful view of
Pongo Pongo and the harbor, but the pollution
caused by large fishing and cruise ships
had darkened and tainted the water. In the
setting of a South Sea paradise, oil scum
and litter really bother you, strike you as
sinfully out of place, totally wrong.

After a sweaty hike north, we glimpsed Vatia from
above—a beautiful, picture-book village, a Shangri-La. The
bay held blue and turquoise water, clear enough to show the

reef below. A few children were running across the white sandy beach, lined with coconut palms and thatched roof huts.

We dashed straight to the water to swim and cool off. Almost immediately a small boy came over and, in good English, said that two girls wanted to meet us. One was his sixteen year old sister, Ipusue'. I wandered over and sat down next to them on the beach.

"Hello. My name is Ipusue' Lilo. Are you thirsty?" She sat with her arms around her knees, and her dark eyes shone.

"Yeah, I am. That was a hot walk."

"I'll get you some water." She and her friend retreated to a thatched roof hut among the palm trees near the edge of the beach. She returned alone, with a big smile and a huge glass.

"What is your name?" She spoke softly, with a strong accent. I told her my name.

"How old are you?" I told her my age.

"Are you married?" Jeez, the way this little beauty got her reference points established in a hurry put my "navigation" to shame.

"No." I laughed, startled at the speed of our negotiations, but unwilling to slow them down.

"Do you have a girlfriend?" She smiled, not very shyly.

"Well, no." For the first time, I lied.

"Do you like me?"

I wish I had stalled a little with something like, "Well, I'd really like to know you better." But instead I played it her way—simple and direct.

"Sure."

"Would you like to marry me?"

"Uh, what?"

Did I hear that right? I couldn't believe it, but, after all, she had followed a pretty logical sequence of questions.

"Would you like to marry me?"

Yup, I'd heard it right. I then made the mistake of assuming Ipusue' was into an interesting South Pacific game. I had heard about island girls, and told myself, she must mean "play married," which sounds like fun. So instead of putting her off with, "That's a little tough to decide before our relationship develops some depth and meaning," I said to myself, what the hell—native hospitality.

"Well, yeah, sure," I told her.

Her smile widened, her eyes joining in. What a beautiful naive young girl. I couldn't wait to see what would happen next.

Ipusue' went back to her fale (house) and I rejoined the crew to wander through the tiny village. Word of the happy union had evidently spread instantly. A woman about forty, the native schoolteacher, approached us, speaking clear English.

"Would you sailors like to stay with me tonight? There is room in the schoolhouse."

Not quite sure it was an innocent offer, we still accepted. As we walked with her she offered several ribald comments and

Wearing our lava lavas in Vatia

suggestions about other possible sleeping arrangements. Her sexual innuendos startled us, but she looked as natural and innocent as a cherub.

"May I give you a shower?" she asked.

What a way with words! After the showers, which she didn't actually give us, she supplied lava lavas to wear. (The women's skirts are puletasis). Feeling silly with those native towels around our waists, we took pictures.

We spent the afternoon on the beach, in the shade, watching preparations for a fia fia (feast)—in our honor, we finally realized. We learned that no other "Europeans" had ever spent a night in the village (not to mention marrying a village girl). Young boys climbed coconut trees to gather the fruit for pulusami, baked coconut in taro leaves. The women pounded cocoa beans to make a drink for special occasions, Samoan Cocoa. For baking, they used umus, outdoor ovens, near the malae, the central court of the village. Next to the village center was the maofa, the chief's house.

At dinnertime, the villagers led us into the large schoolhouse, where we sat on grass mats along the wall. All the furniture, if there had been any, was gone. The elite gathering in the room consisted of the teacher, the old grandmother of the village, the chief, and us. Young girls carried in the food— rice, breadfruit, spam (a rare delicacy in these islands), cocoa, crackers, pulusami, plus other exotic, unrecognizable dishes. Then the room filled up with over thirty villagers, who all sat on the floor against the wall. For several minutes everyone chanted a long Samoan hymn. Then the grandmother offered a seemingly interminable Samoan prayer. After that the special guests and their hosts ate, while everyone else watched. Finally the other poor buggers got to eat.

An impressive formal/informal procedure. I have often wished I could have understood everything said that night, when those loving people offered unknowns like us such strangely moving kindness. They trusted us completely. Treated us as highly honored guests.

After we had eaten, the villagers produced new grass mats and pillows for us to rest on. Then we heard ukulele chords and a pleasing alto singer outside the window—Ipusue', who had been hidden away during the feast. Going outside, I found a full moon reflected in the bay, and a stunning young woman serenading me.

How could such a storybook scene be true? Listening to Ipusue' I leaned against a tree, watching the moon, stars, beach, and ocean, suddenly wondering about Bowditch's claim that one million meteors, bright enough to see, fall from the heavens each hour. I think I was also wondering if anyone else in the world or heavens could be enjoying life as much as I was at that moment. I felt like Tam O'Shanter, the way Robert Burns describes him at his funniest, happiest moment—

> *Kings may be blest, but Tam was glorious,*
> *O'er a' the ills of life victorious!*
> *And like Tam, I would find the happiness all too brief.*
> *For pleasures are like poppies spread;*
> *You seize the bloom, the flower is fled—*
> *Or like the snow upon the river,*
> *A moment white, then gone forever.*

Some sort of sanity reminded me, I really didn't know Ipusue' well enough to marry her. That reluctance soon ruined the party that followed the feast. The entire village population paraded through the trees, dancing, singing. One of Ipusue's brothers came up to me with a rubber knife and poked my chest.

"You're going to marry my sister, aren't you?"

Another one said, "You stay here until the marriage. We will go to Pongo Pongo to get your things off the boat."

I hadn't reckoned on a real marriage, and I hadn't reckoned on real brothers, either. Rapidly, things were getting seriously out of hand. Jack and Dana thought so, too. Their whispered advice was direct and straightforward.

"We better get the hell out of here!"

So we did. I felt terrible—leaving before dawn, not saying goodbye to Ipusue' or the others, taking advantage of their wonderful hospitality, disappointing them, spoiling their celebration. But I couldn't think of another way out. I couldn't very well explain to the entire village I thought "marriage" meant just a good time.

Ipusue' and Vatia haunt me to this day. I remember the beauty of the place, and the beautiful way its people treated me. I still feel guilty about sneaking off in the dark, over the moonlit jungle trail.

Ipusue' had a rough idea of our itinerary, and I did believe I might return someday. I still have a letter she wrote to me, dated July 7, 1973. The envelope, covered with Samoan stamps depicting a crab superimposed over an island, has postmarks from Western Samoa, American Samoa, New Zealand, California, and Idaho. I received it in September.

Ipusue' addressed her message to "Dearest my Boyfriend Dick Williams," and began with a wish for my good health: "Thank to God if you were very well thank you." She had moved to another village in Western Samoa—Salelavalu— and said she wanted me to live there with her.

I want to marry with you because I love you…Dick
I'm not married, I'll wait for you…Please Dick
don't angry with my speaking English. If you found
anything wrong in my letter please my friend Dick
you'll correct it and please Dick may you answer my
letter as quickly as possible?
Wright anything wrong in my letter because I'm not
understand with your own language. That my short
try hard to write a letter with your own language
and please Dick wright the words spelling.
That finished.
Thank You
Good Lucky
Goodbye
Your Own Girl friend

Love Ipusue' Lilo
I love you every time. Don't forget me I want to marry with
you Dick…

Answering Ipusue', and feeling terrible, I tried to explain that our plans had changed and I couldn't return to Samoa.

No wonder everyone hates Americans, if the way I hurt Ipusue' is repeated very often. Anyway, her letter caused me to grow up some and think about the effect of my actions. I was not dealing with islanders of Fletcher Christian's days. But even if those islanders hadn't changed, I should have taken responsibility for my behavior, shouldn't have acted on wild guesses about another, unknown culture.

The island people, full of love and forgiveness, seem to have God's peace and wisdom. A person gets curious, though, about whether they have grown in worldliness.

Surely they have seen other yachts come through. Perhaps my visit wasn't the first time that the whole marriage scene had been enacted. Youth have left the islands in droves since I was there. Maybe I witnessed one way they routinely try to escape.

Looking back, I'm not sure. I'd like to know. It makes a difference.

At the top of the trail to Vatia // Dana and a friend
In the village of Vatia // Native on the jungle trail

10. my favorite island

**We spent two days preparing to sail.
Tom went up the mast in the boatswain's chair
to fix a spreader light, I returned the fuel
system to normal feed from our jury rig, we
fueled, watered, iced, loaded, and stored. The
freezer was permanently shot. As we worked,
I kept glancing up at the tram, and towards
the village of Vatia, expecting any minute
to see Ipusue' Lilo's brothers.**

We set sail in the evening, December 20. We carried some alcohol this time, as we thought we might be at sea during the holidays. Like old salts, even before we lost sight of land, bound for Va Va'U, in the Tongan chain, we were "three sheets to the wind." DJ wanted to move using the genoa sail (50 percent oversize). We obliged him (we thought), and found the *Orpheus* doing eight knots in smooth seas—perfect.

The next morning we paid. A hard heel to starboard and one glance at the jib showed us our drunken mistake of the night before: instead of the genoa we had put up the one sixty-five, fifteen percent larger than the genoa. We next made the mistake of sending forward our prize seaman, Mike, to un-hank the jib. Naturally, he slipped and let go of the halyard.

What he caused by that was a huge pain in the ass as everyone scrambled around the deck trying to catch that swinging son of a bitch while holding our heads. It wrapped itself around everything in sight until we finally caught it, heads pounding, stomachs churning. After that, boredom, a routine sail—until landfall time. Tom navigated the three hundred mile leg with no problems, especially with the math. We caught a lot of Mai Mai, had good wind. Lacking anything important to think about, I made only two discoveries: I was the youngest crew member, and also the only one with brown eyes.

We missed some excitement, as we found out later. The 1972 moon shot touched down in the water only two hundred miles off our course. The astronauts stopped in Pongo Pongo for speeches and celebrations.

To make landfall at some of the Tonga Islands, you don't just casually aim for the harbor. You go through what looks like a maze of fiords, small volcanic islands with a potential for erupting right under you, as I interpret the sailing directions:

> ...*Earth tremors are frequent...specimens of the bottom obtained in sounding around the island show it to be in many places of a volcanic nature... In July 1907, a volcanic eruption was reported to be in progress 30 miles southwestward of the western end of Tongatabu. Caution is necessary when in this neighborhood, and a good lookout kept for any new shoal. In the latter part of 1932 a volcanic eruption was reported in about this position...in 1911 an active volcano was reported in approximately (this area).*

The Tongas differed completely from what I expected, and I have never seen the likes of them anywhere else. The Va Va'U harbor was simple; one long dock, with a few local fishing boats and an old barge. But other landfalls challenge the best of navigators. Entering Neiafu, for example,

> ...pilotage is compulsory...pilots will not take vessels in at night.

On the other hand, pilots will not take vessels in during daylight hours, either, when the beacon lights don't show:

> Owing to the narrow passage southeastward of Galloway Rock, and the fact that the range marks would be astern, a vessel should leave the harbor only in the early forenoon, when the sun is low or at any other time when the light is favorable for seeing the beacons.

When you read the specific instructions, telling you how to zigzag, where to line up with beacons for a turn, what shoals to watch for, and so on, you think you are about to navigate a slalom ski course. H.O. 80, the Sailing Directions, describing the geography and government of the Tonga Islands, report that the group

> ...consists of at least 100 islands and islets; the islands Tongatabu, Eua, and Vavau alone being of any extent...The islands lie generally in a long northward and southward chain...The residence of the sovereign and seat of government is a Nukualofa, in Tongatabu. The population was about 77,429 in 1966...[P]rincipal products are copra and fruit...Tropical cyclones occur...at the rate of about two annually.

When a villager notified Oscar, the governor (and only white man living on the island), that a yacht had arrived, he soon appeared. He occupied a large two-story wooden governor's mansion high on a hill overlooking the beaches and village. The house had an outside upper deck on which we planted ourselves to enjoy Oscar's generous hospitality. He gave us our first "taste" of Australian beer. (The sixteen imperial quarts we downed that afternoon gave us a fair sampling.) Somehow we made it back to the boat that evening, where the local policeman and his brother joined us in further celebration.

Christmas morning arrived quietly. In harbor we would sometimes find it hard to sleep in the passive, unmoving boat. But not that morning. By afternoon we had struggled to life again, ready for a Christmas night that proved unforgettably nourishing. We attended a party on the East side beach—no Hawaiian tourist trap show, but a lavish Tongan feast.

We appreciated a long table full of food, where I soon gravitated toward a large bowl of fruit and fish that you couldn't even recognize as raw and uncooked. Delicious stuff. After feasting, about thirty villagers in festive dress danced and played for several hours in the warm ocean breeze. Then we went swimming in the gentle surf in the dark.

11. deadly paradise

The Bible says rich **people** can **expect trouble**
getting into **heaven—problems like those** of a
camel trying to **pass through the eye** of a **needle.**

The un-rich crew of *Orpheus* faced "needle's eye" trouble
the day after Christmas, trying to enter a watery paradise.
None of us will likely forget the adventure. A mixture of
delight and terror, claustrophobia and discovery.

The experience began when new friends—locals we had
met the night before—took us out in a small outboard to
Mariner's and Swallows' caves. (Legend had it that a Tongan
princess had once been kidnapped and hidden in Swallows'

cave.) On the ocean surface only a round rock about fifty feet high marks the location, several miles from the main island.

The locals instructed us to dive down two fathoms, swim underwater through a hole in the rock for one fathom (about the length of a body!), then surface. Because of their limited English and our own secret terror at performing such a maneuver without scuba gear, we had our hosts repeat their directions several times. They looked on our hesitancy with humor.

We took numerous preliminary dives, first searching for the hole, then trying to peer through it. The combined distance down and in stretched our lung capacity. After each unsuccessful surfacing we would find the Tongans laughing, urging us on. Could these jovial, innocent folk be tricking us, like some evil twisted characters in a horror movie? We would rest on the gunwales of the boat, catching our breath for the next descent, nervously parrying the natives' impatient motions to get on with it.

Another concern had given us pause: if we went all the way in and couldn't get air, backing out and up would become quite important very quickly. What if, by that time, we had passed the point of no return, no more backup? In this battle between claustrophobia and the spirit of adventure, maybe pride finally outweighed fear.

Finally, we succeeded! After feeling the walls of the tunnel closing in, and once more keenly recognizing my need for new air, I suddenly popped out into a high-ceiling cave with water about sixty feet deep. Swallows flew all around. I imagined a beautiful princess up on the rocks in the corner.

Relieved, repentant of my ugly, anxiety-born suspicions, I felt a rush of goodwill toward these generous secret-sharers, these good-humored people who again had proved themselves to be perfect hosts.

Occupants of the well-named Friendly Islands love to offer gifts; we had already benefited from encounters with them as they sat outside their huts, working at food, clothing, or jewelry projects. As we would start to walk by they would smile and motion us over, to hand over anything that happened to catch our eye. (I quit admiring things after a while, even though the Tongans didn't seem to mind that we had very little to exchange.) I received shell necklaces, a triton, a giant clam shell, and lots of exotic native delicacies—fruits and seafood, mostly.

On this trip their gift would be memorable swimming adventures. After letting us enjoy for a time our triumph over the caves, our hosts next led us to a scuba diver's dream world. We went out to an underwater reef where, at eighty feet, the water almost matched surface temperature. No thermal layer. It afforded visibility of at least one hundred fifty feet. And in spite of its delights, I was to learn, it contained deadlier dangers than Swallows' cave did.

The reef seemed anchored to the other side of the world, or maybe just as far down as hell. Eighty-five feet looked and felt like forty. In fact I could hardly believe the depth gauge when I looked. After our first dive the guys snorkeling above said they had seen us and we looked about an inch long.

Jack and I took pictures of each other, then got down to serious sightseeing. Jack concentrated on life forms in the coral, while I watched, fascinated, scores of iridescent green parrot fish the size of my hand, and thousands of butterfly fish, swimming in formation.

Suddenly something jerked me violently around. Immediately, out of my subconscious fears came the nightmarish thought that some huge sea beast had seized me. Finding only Jack at first gave momentary relief—plus minor irritation. But those reactions turned to horror when I saw why Jack had grabbed me. A deadly Coral Sea snake had come up behind me; Jack had probably saved my life by pulling me away. Had the serpent bitten me, I would have died rapidly and painfully, with no antidote for the poison.

That nearly fatal encounter put a damper on the rest of the dive. I didn't have much air left anyway, and spent my time trying to look over both shoulders. Later, over a beer, Jack and I talked briefly about the episode, never really acknowledging its importance or paying him the gratitude he deserved.

A policeman friend took me to the Kava House (Ava in Samoan), a large smoky tavern with the flavor of an opium den. The patrons—all men except for one woman behind the bar—sat at a large rectangular table in the middle of the room, seventeen of us, all ages. In a huge wooden bowl (tanoa) the woman was mixing kava, a milky-looking liquid made from ground pepper, tree roots, and water.

She placed it in front of the oldest man, across from me. He dipped a coconut shell bowl in, filled it, and passed it to his left. It went clear around the table to the man on his right, who drank the whole bowlful without stopping, then acknowledged the old man, perhaps a chief, with a nod and a few words (manuia). A sprinkle of kava was tossed under a mat as an offering to the gods, then "soifua," and down the hatch. Women could evidently only tap the bowl with their fingers as a sign of respect.

When my turn came it took tremendous effort to drink the whole bowlful without gagging. Though it tastes like bitter warm sour coconut milk, kava, a narcotic drink, actually comes from tree roots.

The first cup hypnotized me. I couldn't move. After the second cup I couldn't talk. The third cup made a zombie of me—a zombie frustrated as hell, because the old man next to me was talking about navigating using only stars and wind, no charts, compass, or sextant. I desperately wanted to understand what he was saying, but the combination of language barrier and kava left his meaning totally unreachable.

In this mind-hammering high, I got back to the boat eventually, but don't remember how. I eventually realized why I had seen men sitting outside the building during the day in a bloodshot trance. At least they escaped by their own devices. Plenty of other problems were entirely the white man's fault.

The lasting gifts of the first white sailors were syphilis, other diseases, and alcohol. According to my old journal, I wondered if the missionaries hadn't been more destructive, in the long run, than the first sailors. One "gift" of the missionaries, the sense of guilt, deprived the natives of their happy innocent nudity, their cultural traditions, and natural ways and thoughts that can never be retrieved. I wrote,

Even the current missionaries keep the natives under tight control, shaping them into just what the churches want. What Western churches have done and continue to do has created sin out of innocence. These islands have lost much of the freedom that God gave them, thanks to the white man.

12. serious navigation— mariner and pilot

My last day in Nieafu was spent "navigating," planning for daylight passage to Tongatapu, a tough 180-mile sail among rocks, wrecks, atolls, atollons, fringing reefs, barrier reefs, and vigias.

The H.O. sailing directions warned me that each of the foregoing has its hazards, and I spent a lot of thoughtful time with the books reading about the problems—vigias in the area, for instance—

reported shoals whose existence or exact locality is doubtful. In no part of the world are there so many dangerous coral reefs and low islets rising abruptly from great depths as in the Pacific Ocean; in addition, a vast number of vigias have from time to time been reported. Many of these have been disproved in late years by laborious research, but many are still on the charts; and until the existence of doubtful shoals has been disproved, they must remain a source of anxiety and perplexity to the navigator…The appearance of vigias, sometimes caused by reflection from the clouds, by volcanic disturbance, by shoals of fish, and by marine animalcule, often resemble reefs and breakers so closely as to deceive the most experienced.

The directions make you aware of the vital importance of direct eyeballing:

> *Navigation among coral reefs…is often dependent upon the eye… reefs…are always more plainly to be seen from the masthead than from the deck or bridge; when the sun is high rather than when it is low; when the sun is behind the observer rather than facing him; and when the sea is slightly ruffled. If the sea is glassy calm it is extremely difficult to distinguish reefs.*

All such information as the above demanded respect. We faced such a tough sail, in fact, that DJ planned to navigate it himself, with my help. I looked forward to assisting him, learning some new navigational tricks.

In preparation, I enjoyed figuring times, distances, and headings for the different legs to route us around hazards. I knew that the more I prepared, the more I'd profit from

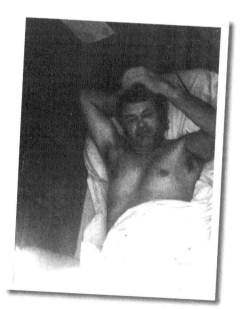

DJ's corrections and advice. Timing for daylight passage, a critical factor, would challenge us navigators to make constant adjustments en-route.

With the crew all packed and ready to go, and me feeling extremely thankful for the backup I would get, DJ suddenly got sick with a bad case of flu or food poisoning.

DJ relaxes in the quarter bunk

At first I suspected him of faking it in order to give me some kind of test, but one look at him convinced me otherwise. He looked terrible. He also looked worried.

I suggested staying in port until DJ felt better. He said no, let's go do it. So? The Fates had just handed me a baby to save, an unplanned test to pass. The Gipper had just told me to win a Big One for him and Notre Dame.

We had scarcely left the quay when a squall moved in from behind us, dropping visibility nearly to zero— right in the midst of a maze of fjords and islets. I wanted to turn around, but couldn't see behind, and couldn't judge the size of the squall.

A visual-rated pilot, unexpectedly immersed in clouds, would feel about the way I did then—if, in addition, he has no radar or instrument-reading skills, and if his last glimpse of nearby mountaintops showed them looming higher than his plane. He would figure his chances of staying alive to be a little dim.

As for me at that moment, I just grimly held my calculated compass heading—easy with the wind pushing from behind. Luckily the squall soon died down enough to give us visibility again. From the helm I could watch DJ lying on the quarter berth in the cabin, and he could watch me. After the *Orpheus'* recovery from blindness, DJ no doubt shared the relief he saw in my eyes and body.

Once we got into more open water, we hit a ten-foot chop and twenty-five knot gusty winds. After double-reefing the main and setting our smallest jib (we didn't have a real storm jib), we still made seven to eight knots. I settled in, expecting a long day, a bit more excitement, and more heavy weather. I should also have anticipated a very edgy crew throughout the whole goddam leg.

Because the weather, in fact, permitted only two sextant shots that day, our survival would depend critically on dead reckoning—all the more difficult with no taffrail log to estimate speed through the water.

I spent hours studying pilot charts. Making no less than eight course changes, all dead reckoned, we saw dozens of small islets, volcanoes, reefs, breakers, and wrecks, all along the way.

At five p.m. Tom sighted three islands where we were supposed to find only two. I just about crapped. I also felt an immediate loss of confidence in me by the crew. DJ might have been an exception.

But a few minutes later the "third island" disappeared, and I got a positive fix before dark—a crucially needed clue for changing course and steering around a wreck and exposed rock.

My reputation steadily improved until about eleven p.m., the time of Dana's dismaying discovery. He spotted a light dead ahead.

Everyone, including DJ, crowded up to look. Now even my teacher had his doubts. Eyeing me, in front of everyone he said,

"You better go down there and do some **serious** navigating, pal."

Shattered and scared, I asked myself, What in the hell have I done wrong? I rechecked everything—headings, current, drift, speed—and nothing connected. It didn't make sense. I was going over it for the third time when someone on deck realized that the light came from a boat, one probably also bound for Tongatabu.

After that I briefly tried to sleep, and twice the rough seas dashed water on my bunk from an unsealed hatch. I spent most of the night reading sailing directions and checking figures.

At three a.m. Tom saw another ship heading our way. I spied land at seven a.m., on schedule and on course. I felt exhausted, but triumphant.

Then things got worse.

I had underestimated the difficulty of getting into harbor, and we didn't even have a harbor chart. Besides the seasonal threat of "sudden and violent" squalls, the sailing directions warned that

> *the passage between Tongatabu and Nomuka is dangerous because of uncharted shoals... westward of Tongatabu...is a small reef...600 yards in length north and south and 500 yards east and west...a formidable danger to vessels approaching this part of the coast on a dark night...The North Coast...is very broken and low...coral reefs extend some distance from the shore and for 9 miles to the northward. Numerous small islands and islets are scattered about on the reef, amid which are the approaches to the chief port and anchorage...*

Three channels led to the anchorage, the sailing directions reported. Only one, the "Lahi Passage," had the book's grudging recommendation—or rather, least disfavor.

> *Vessels entering this channel are cautioned to keep within the dragged area...the bottom shoals rapidly in this vicinity and dangerous coral heads may exist undetected in water that has been sounded and appears to be clear of obstructions...[The instructions*

*name three deadly reefs, plus a hazardous wreck.
Therefore,]...Pilotage is compulsory for merchant
vessels.*

Where was that compulsory pilotage when we needed it?
I found myself thinking of a little gem from my Grandmother
Fern's "notebook of sayings," *The wise young mariner takes the
pilot on board and has a compass, chart, and stars. He finds
freedom and the true harbor of his soul.*

Maybe the author was speaking in mystical parallels, and
meant something pretty spiritual as "pilot." But this young
mariner, far from wise, couldn't have wished harder for flesh
and blood guidance, as well as paper and ink guidance—a
harbor chart.

When I saw three different points of land and couldn't
decide which led to the harbor entrance, I woke DJ up. I had
had enough.

DJ had almost recovered by then. He put Tom up the
mast in the boatswain's chair to watch from above, while Jack
took the helm and DJ stood on the bow. I went below to
work on the engine, which had picked one hell of a time to
start overheating.

As we got closer, two fishermen in a small dingy saw us
and began waving and yelling. They told us we were headed
right for the reef.

So we **did** get our pilot when we needed him. One
fisherman got on board to graciously guide us in. We tied up
at noon. (It could have been a little sooner, if Tom and Dana
had remembered how to do bowlines.)

We did the usual quick island check-out: beer, girls, and
ice cream. A dance scheduled for that night sounded inviting,

but after a freshwater shower I turned in for seventeen hours of sleep. When I finally woke up I felt tempted to make a little sign for myself that would read,

Dick Williams

Young Mariner and Journeyman Navigator

13. endings and beginnings

On the next day, the last of the year, the
famous Tongan king Taufaahau (or "Tupou"—
who weighed three hundred sixty-five pounds)
invited us and the only other yachter in harbor
to the New Year's Eve party at his palace.

Before the bash, DJ and I managed to borrow the
required ties and jackets and arrived at the party in high spirits,
riding double on the mini-bike right up to the palace lawn.
A hell of a good start for a fine party. Somewhat surprisingly,
we never did get booted out for rowdiness. I don't remember
much about the king or crown prince, except a kind of jolly
and open-minded hospitality.

In this free-for-all gala, DJ really laid on an extra helping
of charm, and everyone loved him.

An ancient amazing tortoise named Tuimalila resided
in the palace gardens. In 1772 Captain Cook had given him
to an ancestor of Queen Salote's. Though a fire had blinded
him, and a car had struck and dented his shell, Tuimalila
continued to waddle around, a real survivor.

* * *

As 1973 arrived, I remember thinking that I had been
looking for freedom, and seemed now to be on the way to

finding it. On my own, traveling the world, no ties to bind, I had few regrets, little to feel bad about—but not very much to feel good about, either. Freedom had brought little else with it.

Soon my focus would shift from "freedom" to "responsibility"—which I got more of than I bargained for. Learning about things like rules, craziness, growth, wearying fright, and the laws of nature and humanity would became more important in 1973.

And losses—the New Year would be handing me several of those, beginning with my good friend Tom.

I guess a rift had been coming for some time.

A serious smoker during his college years, Tom habitually consumed two packs of cigarettes a day—non-filtered Camels, on prosperous days. When cash was low he fell back on home-rolled Bugler. Aboard the *Orpheus*, Tom decided to quit, and perhaps his tortured nerves figured in as a factor in some of our flare-ups.

I still remember him at Berkeley—the center of a bluish cloud, smiling, shirt sleeves undone and unrolled, blue eyes piercing, ever-present cigarette dangling between fingers, leaving a smoke trail as he expounded on philosophy, culinary arts, or whatever.

We had had a role-reversal. No longer a student (almost a disciple) of his, I found myself disagreeing with him on a number of issues, beginning with DJ. Tom and some others thought DJ had ripped us off; $1,300 apiece seemed too much to them for room, board, and travel, plus sailing and navigation lessons to New Zealand and back. We also knew, vaguely, that the Coast Guard had some laws about charter boating that DJ might have disregarded or violated.

I didn't have a problem with either point. I thought the price fair—cheap, even—for what we were getting. I figured DJ had a captain's license, or equivalent experience and expertise. And we had left Coast Guard waters behind.

We also differed in that Tom and the others hadn't fallen in love with sailing. As novices we had begun with similar feelings about the romance of the sea, similar background reading encounters with Long John Silver, jolly rogers, shipwrecks, buried treasures, Robinson Crusoe, Christian and The Bounty. Our South Seas expectations included leisurely moments on a flat deck, cocktails in hand, dolphins, a lingering sunset, beautiful naked island women anxious to please, swimming to the boat.

But life on the *Orpheus* had taught us to interweave those images with the realities of storms, sickness, bad food, no privacy, and claustrophobia. We experienced some of the pretty, more of the grubby.

Given a chance to escape, most of the crew would take it, as later events were to prove. But something different had happened to me, something that has affected no more than two percent of all the shipmates I ever knew: the sea gets into your blood. By New Years it was in mine.

We had become conscious of our differences on that point. Tom had done fine at sea, but he found it too limiting to satisfy his kind of pilgrim, endlessly searching for a better life somewhere. (But what could ever totally please a man who called himself both an idealist and an existential pessimist?)

He came on board one day and threw a tantrum, calling us all slobs, ordering everyone to clean up the boat. Knowing Tom to be the biggest messer in the galley, we could have laughed off the outburst and chalked it up as a nicotine fit;

but Jack laid into him so fiercely I felt embarrassed for them both.

I didn't escape Tom's tongue-lashings, either. I could stay good-humored about most things, but when he lit into me about a Berkeley woman I had been close to—Renee', a beautiful singer—he made me furious. Tom knew how passionately I hoped for a future with her, and decided to give me a dose of reality. He let me down hard.

Renee' and I had been writing to each other. When I mentioned to Tom my missing her, my wish for a letter, he suddenly lowered the boom on me, seizing on the point that my correspondence was destined to lead nowhere.

"Do you really think Renee' would leave her private-eye husband, six Arabian Salukis, two Citroens, a house in the redwoods, and her high social connections, for a twenty-two year old slob who's never done anything? Wake up!"

I had been already feeling insecure about the whole situation. That question destroyed me. It also angered me as another revelation of Tom's changing attitude that made him willing to put me down on personal matters. The growing adversarial atmosphere included rivalry in sailing and navigation as well as everyday life. Maybe I helped create the competition; I must have. But I hadn't known it, and never meant to do that. I tried to talk, the way we used to, but he wouldn't. It blew me away. He had **always** talked. He was deeply pissed about something.

I wanted to believe that Tom's break from smoking had mostly caused our problem. But I was seeing the beginning of a permanent end to a friendship that had done much to help me grow up.

While we were still in Tonga, tropical storm Elinore birthed north of Samoa, heading our way. We set extra anchors and stern spring lines from our boat, about ten feet from the shore. These crossed lines kept us from going any direction without holding us too tight. The storm was going force eight to nine, touching ten. It passed us to the east and south, but caused some excitement for awhile.

To get ashore, we would swing on a line tied to the spinnaker pole, rigged ninety degrees to the deck. The chances of a dry landing were about 60 percent. The "launching line" provided the fun of watching someone almost make it to shore, almost make it back to the boat. The victim's swing would peter out over the water midway—leaving him kicking, hopelessly ocean-bound.

I spent January third getting fuel, checking weather, reading, and tracing a borrowed harbor chart. (I didn't want any future *Orpheus* navigator to face the kind of panic I felt entering a dangerous harbor with no pilot and no chart.) Tom repaired the mainsail at reef and batten points.

We all wanted to weigh anchor, having actually grown bored with Tongatabu. We didn't like its atmosphere, hadn't made good friends among people that seemed too tourist-wise and cynical. I decided the place hadn't been worth the pain of getting to it. (Va Va'U turned out to be my favorite

island, Tongatabu my least favorite.)

I happened to meet, though, the most interesting individual in the vicinity—John Riding, master of the *Sea Egg,* the only other sailboat in the harbor. This amazing twelve-foot homemade sloop from England, with only six-foot, four inch John Riding aboard, was circling the world. Riding had been at it eight years, had written two books, had been through three hurricanes and a "pitch-poll" (in which a boat does a somersault). Listening to him, I was bug-eyed. He used a handheld compass, like a Boy Scout pathfinder but about fifty years older and almost impossible to read, and he used longhand algebraic navigation, just for kicks. His immaculate chart work showed beautiful clear notations. I couldn't fathom how he did it in that tiny boat.

I spent my last evening in Tonga with John, on board the *Sea Egg.* He made seafood curry, I bought the beer. He intended to stop next in Auckland, as we did, and we planned a reunion. I found myself talking to him about my grandfather and the old sailing ways. How my grandfather was the only person in Denver who could splice the old elevator cables, both wire to wire and wire to rope. And how he could box the compass in less than a minute, from memory:

N, N by E, NNE, NE by N, NE, NE by E, ENE, E
by N, E, E by S, ESE, SE by E, SE, SE by S, SSE,
S by E, S, S by W, SSW, SW by S, SW, SW by W,

*Tom **looked** the same*

WSW, W by S, W, W by N, WNW, NW by W, NW, NW by N, NNW, N by W, N.

Thirty-two points.

I never saw John Riding again. I tried to check on him, but no one I met in New Zealand knew of his existence. He seemed invincible, but I discovered years later that he was lost somewhere in the Tasman Sea after landing in the north part of New Zealand. Neither he nor his boat was ever seen again.

* * *

Twelve hundred fifty miles from Tonga to Auckland, our next planned destination.

As we left harbor, Tom, then navigating, misread my harbor chart tracing and damn near put us on the reef first thing. Wouldn't ever admit his mistake; and I refused to concede my chart might be hard to interpret. More signs of deteriorating friendship.

Smoke began pouring out the hatches about then, caused by a scuba backpack shorting out a battery. I scrambled for a fire extinguisher—unnecessary at that time, as it happened, but good practice for the future. A few days later we had starter problems we traced to a bad solenoid. Then an exhaust leak began to stink up the boat. (As a sailor, I feel compelled to complain that engines are a pain in the ass. Using them, you can only hope for the best and learn to expect the worst.)

We saw our first phosphorus in the water, eerie and beautiful. Millions of white sparkles in the bow wave, with dolphins joyously jumping through them. One night an albatross smacked our backstay with a huge bang, causing permanent damage to the bird and more than temporary anxiety among superstitious crew members.

Another night, when all of us suddenly felt freezing cold, we checked the thermometer: seventy-two degrees. We were leaving the tropics.

Swinging to shore in Tonga

14. end of the line: New Zealand

**We had a one hundred forty-eight mile day,
smooth seas, and the southern sky—
a one-out-of-nine perfect sailing day.**

We also saw our first marlin, and lots of albatross. Porpoise sightings, too. And to top it all, the Green Flash.

Bowditch owlishly describes the phenomenon in great detail—beginning with a background cause, prismatic refraction of sunlight in the earth's atmosphere, producing different colors:

Since the amount of bending is slightly different for each color, separate images of the sun are formed in each color of the spectrum. The effect is similar to that of imperfect color printing in which the various colors are slightly out of register. However, the difference is so slight that the effect is not usually noticeable.

The greatest spreading of refracted colors takes place at the horizon, about one-sixth of a degree between the violet and red bands of the spectrum. The setting sun appears to travel that distance in about two-thirds of a second.

The red image, being bent least by refraction, is first to set and last to rise. The shorter wave blue and violet colors are scattered most by the atmosphere, giving it its characteristic blue color. Thus, as the sun sets, the

green image may be the last of the colored images to
drop out of sight. If the red, orange, and yellow images
are below the horizon, and the blue and violet light
is scattered and absorbed, the upper rim of the green
image is the only part seen, and the sun appears green.
This is the green flash.

In his *The Lonely Sea and The Sky*, Sir Francis Chichester offered a more poetic account, after seeing the green flash through binoculars, magnified seven times:

When next I looked at the Texas Tower I saw the
three white doves standing high above the horizon on
long stilted legs—a mirage. I had a fascinating view
through my binoculars of the sun setting. Because of
the mirage, it looked like an untidy heap of red-hot
metal dumped on the horizon. Gradually it flattened
and widened and as it disappeared I was able to see
the famous green flash magnified seven times.

We saw only one green flash, but that's all it takes to be forever looking for another.

If it weren't for bad we'd never recognize good, as the weather the next night reminded us. What we thought to be just another squall hit at three a.m. When they come in the dark the first thing you notice is total blackness, then a subtle change in wind velocity, along with the smell of rain. Occasionally lightning strikes, giving enough light to show dark, swirling clouds down low. A handy, alert helmsman will have shortened sail by this time, or asked for help. If he hasn't, everyone generally comes out anyway, because the high-pitched wind and the boat's heeling have made even the slowest landlubber conscious—and uncomfortable.

During the passage of the squall, which usually takes ten or fifteen minutes, the wind sometimes shifts in a three hundred-sixty-degree circle. To avoid tack changes, we would simply follow the wind around the circle. And as it passed, the trades would miraculously resume, the sky would lighten a little, and on our way we would go.

This three a.m. squall, though, represented frontal activity, which meant a longer curse. We passed the date line in a short choppy sea that upset a person's equilibrium. Everyone eventually got sick except me, and I took over Tom's job of navigating. Remembering my bet with Dana, I silently thanked my forebears for salty blood, a strong stomach, and luck.

On January 14th New Zealand appeared, 4,500 miles from Honolulu. Landfall came early in the morning, and we sailed among the locals all day to dock that evening in Auckland. Showing off, we hoisted the banana staysail, did some wing and wing (sailing downwind with the jib and mainsail on opposite beams), and every other stunt we could think of. Lots of weekend sailors watched us curiously, studying our United States and quarantine flags.

Our performance had an anticlimactic ending in Auckland's notoriously shallow harbor. After clearing customs and heading for a yacht club slip, as directed, we drove the *Orpheus* right into the mud. We loosened up and cleaned up, then headed into town for a celebration dinner and party. As we watched, a little awestruck, our DJ continued to impress the locals—this time, as an American Don Juan. He turned on the charm, and in almost no time had female company.

We all shared a natural high, based on a feeling of accomplishment. We had actually come all that way.

Part 2: Travels in Kiwiland

1. country boy on the prowl

**Getting off the boat and away from me
made Tom cheerful, close to ecstatic.**

Before heading out of town we had lunch together in a park—a strained session. We never bothered to discuss traveling together; out of the question, by unspoken agreement. In contrast with his earlier volatile behavior, Tom remained calm, but a sad, resigned air took the place of his recent good humor. Our friendship had vanished—not suddenly or cleanly, but finally. Tom didn't really like me anymore.

I got some comfort from the fairly thick packet of letters waiting for me—but not much. The woman I most wanted to hear from hadn't written.

New Zealand stamps

DJ, pursuing his dream of a seventy-two foot racing boat, was hanging around in Auckland, hobnobbing with world-class shipwrights. (Almost everyone in the three New Zealand islands has water transportation of some kind. That boat owners market has attracted some of the best builders and designers in the world.) I obviously didn't fit in with DJ's new crowd.

Maybe the time had come to try some personal therapy—make it on my own for a while, deal with a threatened identity crisis. Maybe just lose myself in a land like California in latitude and size, but more cut off from the world. (In 1973 it held a population of only three million; the sheep outnumbered the people.)

So I headed out, on my own, to meet a few of those three million persons—and maybe have a few conversations with myself. I had five weeks.

Quiet country roads can give you a free and easy feeling, just walking along, enjoying solitude, thinking about the future, putting the past behind, coming to terms with uncertainties like love and friendship. I did some hitch-hiking, too, of course, which occasionally produced the very opposite effects.

One day I was innocently riding in the front seat of an old van that had a regular glass windshield. The rear tire of a passing truck hurled a rock backwards, which instantly and totally destroyed our "windscreen."

The sound, like a fifty-bulb chandelier falling on cement, almost deafened us. Fortunately, the damage to our faces didn't compare with the damage to the wind-shield. Moments like that don't exactly settle your nerves.

A more prolonged life-threatening situation lay ahead of me in the "Southern Alps" region, but before I got that

far, a month of meandering had helped in sorting out a lot of problems and uncertainties, and in getting reoriented.

New Zealand offered me at least a passing acquaintance with its amazing, bright, mysterious Maori—one of them, in fact, became a longtime friend. A story of the ESP of Maori voodoo doctors had been circulating just before I arrived in New Zealand.

A scuba diver had disappeared near New Plymouth. After a futile ten-day official search, the diver's family consulted a Maori voodoo doctor who told them exactly where to find the dead man's remains. Suspicious, they consulted another voodoo a hundred and fifty miles away, and got the same story, the same pinpointed location. Both voodoos described an underwater cave a hundred yards from the body where, they said, a giant octopus resided.

After those directions had led divers directly to the victim, no one would attempt a dive inside the cave to recover the scuba gear.

I've read about what nineteenth century people called "the wander year," in which a young man who had finished formal schooling would just take off and travel for a time before settling down to a permanent job. Maybe the nineteenth century wasn't so dumb. Every young person probably needs time alone and some perspective to deal

A steam locomotive on South Island

with the crises of growing up in a strange world, wondering how you will ever fit into it, what you will do to survive. If more young people had gotten things out of their system, had tested their preferences and dislikes, perhaps later, as middle-aged folks, more of them would be leading happier lives. Instead, they went straight from school to marriage and children, with, critically, no time for and with themselves.

Anyway, traveling in New Zealand alone for a few weeks probably made a difference in my later life. I learned three things especially about my own preferences: (1) country beats city; (2) when you get tired of solitude, kids like those of New Zealand—easy-going, natural, friendly—are great to mingle with; (3) flying an airplane beats almost any other diversion.

I rented a plane in Christchurch a couple of times, badly straining my wallet to buy a little consolation and excitement. Though mountain climbing can leave me clinging to a ledge of rock like a scared fledgling bird, actual flying gives a totally different feeling. You move, you soar—alone, free, detached. Immersed in air, not just teetering on a cliff between earth and sky. I didn't know it then, but I had found my vocation.

2. the routeburn

"DECEMBER" (PART 6 & 7)
I can tell you what it is
To be lost
In the mountains: reticence
Of trees and the hard
Rush of water.

Deeper and deeper in,
The stream taking you
A strange way. Feet
In the water,
You slip from the dark
Side of stones.
Afraid. The gentle
Teeth of the fern
Have eaten your
Going back.

You ask the way at each
Turning, and are answered
Birch, basswood,
Water over a rock.

This is lawyer's weather.
A dog digs for cold bones.
Rock salt runs a fever
Cutting down to the stones.

Certainty has a price:
We notarize our wives.
Sweet Mother of Christ,
Let the sun rise.

—*Conrad Hilberry*

On New Zealand's South Island, several backpacking trails cross the Southern Alps from the eastern plains to the west coast fiord lands. One of the most popular of these, the Routeburn Track, runs some twenty miles over fantastic country. Beginning in deeply-wooded canyons and ravines, it leads above the timber line, past craggy, rugged rocks and peaks—often hidden and teased by ragged fog and wind. It provides landscapes and scenes not unlike those you imagine in *The Hobbit.* Enchanting, mysterious.

In Queenstown I had met Sandra, an Australian redhead who seemed to exist on another plane, one where peace and calm reign. We had known each other less than an hour when she decided to join me for the Routeburn trek. Something about her personal mystique made me fantasize that we had known each other for a much longer time in some other dimension.

She woke me early the next morning and we headed for Glenarchy, where the road ended. The river looked too deep to wade, but we found a boat going across later that day. Sandra slept leaning on my shoulder as we waited. She was young, (we both were, I guess) maybe innocent, but so imperturbable, so serene she seemed wise. Perhaps that's what got us into trouble later—she soothed me to the point of neglecting even the basic preparation for overland travel in the wilderness. Maybe an independent way of traveling at sea in the *Orpheus* also had numbed me to the dangers of the Routeburn.

(Any reasonably experienced hiker and camper would have known better, and I should have. I never believed in frills, but even the hardiest survivalist could hardly call walking shoes, food, and sturdy clothing "frills.")

On the other side of the river we met Harry Bryant, who gave us a ride to his lodge at the trailhead. Sixty-four-and-a-half years old, Harry had lived there all his life. My companion's otherworldly powers must have influenced him to let us stay in the old lodge building, by ourselves, for no charge. A glorious setting. I noticed his blue eyes looking wistfully at Sandra.

We built a fire, I took an ice bath in the river, and we ate toasted cheese and tea for dinner. We listened to packrats in the dark.

The next day we took the climb to Routeburn Falls. I tried fishing with green stick, string, pin, and worm, with no luck. Even if we had found our way to hobbit land, the Ring in our minds worked no magic, and someone must have called Gandolf the Wizard away to another land.

But we did discover the Friendly Forest, filled with thick moss-covered, dew-dripping trees with gnarled twisted ancient branches hiding the sun. The trail tunneled into a dark unknown. With time on hold, the day could just as well have been a month.

The hut at the falls offered us the comfort and diversion of listening to rain and Kea birds on the roof. What should worry us about the trail ahead? Sandra's rubber thongs were holding up (she had left her boots in Christchurch). In our (unrealistic) opinion, our supplies of one loaf of bread, a chunk of cheese, a pound of raisins, six oranges, and some tea, would easily last us.

After lunch, Sandra convinced me we should leave the hut and forge ahead, despite rain, fog, and stern warnings that in such weather hikers should not attempt a summit crossing on the poorly marked trail.

How did she do that? Did she possess some kind of
mountain Siren, mind-bending powers, or am I just making
far-fetched excuses for my own bad planning? How could a
tenderfoot explain himself, much less a veteran? I can only
stupidly repeat that this girl somehow made me believe there
was nothing to worry about. To children of nature, nature
would provide.

We left the hut about two p.m. I didn't want to go. I
argued. I was happily reading, writing, and napping. But we
left. After five minutes we realized that we had a hard climb
ahead. Within a quarter of an hour we were sloshing along a
trail that had turned into an ice cold creek about eight inches
deep.

Sandra began to really amaze me then. A childlike person
who didn't even know how to whine, she **never** complained.
She could appreciate the beauty of a place or a spot in time,
even while miserably cold and drenched. Her feet numb,
she bravely trudged along in her thongs. Throughout an
adventure that called on all her reserves, she never doubted
that both of us would emerge relatively unscathed.

We came to a split in the trail, not shown on the map.
We followed the path marked by a large orange arrow. Then
Sandra's thong broke. We might have made it if that hadn't
happened. (But really, how could we have **not** expected a
$1.98 thong to break on a three-day mountain hike?)

I repaired the thong with string and my knife. About
a third of a mile later we hit what appeared to be a dead
end on a small rocky knoll, at the head of a trail that had
become a creek. We got no help from my now uselessly soggy
paper map. We turned back towards the split in the trail,
Sandra showing early signs of hypothermia. (I hadn't heard

that term back then. I called it shock or "some kind of altered consciousness.")

A short way up the other trail a large over-hanging boulder offered us shelter. I brought Sandra up under it with instructions to stay and rub her feet and hands. I ran ahead another quarter mile or so, to try to identify the trail, fighting an all-too-familiar sense of panic. The rain pounded down fiercely, cold as ice. The fog had reduced visibility to almost nil. Being above the timberline, we had no landmarks, but when the trail became clearer, I decided we **must** have chosen the right one. I ran back to Sandy who had just been standing like a depressed statue, motionless.

I madly sat her down and put her feet in my armpits—both of us cold and wet to numbness. I gave her my wool hat, ski gloves, scarf, wool sweater, wool socks, and boots, and kept two pairs of wool socks, no shoes.

Leaving her again at what I thought must be Harris Saddle, the

Sandra contemplates

most exposed, dangerous part of the trail, I went slopping up the wet trail in my socks as fast as I could. Sandy was to follow slowly, while I looked ahead for the emergency shelter at the summit, our only hope. We had no other plan, no other out.

In such a state, with no resources, no solutions, and you think time is running out, you can hardly fight off panic. It wells up in your chest. The heart rate increases, revs up your defense systems, screws up your brain.

Mind games can run wild. You can lose the ability to sort out plans and make right decisions. Fear can disrupt every rational effort. You fight off fright to work out a plan, then panic takes over again and you forget all but pieces of the strategy.

In a cockpit, or a sailboat, panic can do deadly damage. On earth, you have more of a chance. Time means less. You can at least still plod along while you panic.

My mind, a complete mess, had me both cursing Sandy for making us leave the hut, while admiring her spunk; had me worrying about the danger of frostbite or shock, distracted by reminders to maintain feeling in my feet, puzzled about our location, dreading the approach of darkness and life-threatening cold, wondering how all this could possibly be happening with someone I hardly knew.

I rounded a turn, looked up, and suddenly saw an orange tent peeking through the fog ahead. I ran up to it and to my amazement found a doctor and his son inside the emergency shelter we had been looking for, a ten by twelve foot rigid plastic tent.

"Dad, Dad, look, 'e's in 'is stocking feet, 'e is! 'e hasn't got 'is bloody boots on!"

"Yeah, kid. When your socks get a little ripe you wash and wear them."

I had seen this little brat before, back at the Routeburn Falls hut, where he had specialized in leaving the door open—a practice he was to maintain religiously at the summit shelter also.

We weren't complaining this time. The doc cooked a hot meal on his backpack stove and checked Sandra out. In a model of British understatement, he said, well, yes, we had been rather fortunate in finding shelter when we had.

Later, I even obligingly talked American politics with the inquisitive doctor—the last thing I wanted to discuss that evening. But Sandra and I owed him dearly—and she had little to contribute to the doctor's subject of interest.

Sandra and I both slept poorly. I dreamt of old disappointments—a time in Berkeley when a heroin addict stole most of my personal belongings, and a more recent time, when Tom had made me understand Renee's probable rejection of me. With the moon visible through the breaking storm, lighting Harris Lake below us and the rocky peaks above, I got up and stood outside a long time that night, as I had enjoyed doing at sea. I recalled a strangely peaceful episode before Sandra and I reached the shelter. In our miserable, dangerously exposed position, we had momentarily stood marveling at lake scenery and the beautiful, changing skies.

Another time, on the wrong trail, Sandra had turned around (I was following to catch her in case she slipped), and pointed at the water hole she had just stepped into. With a hilarious look of amazement and disbelief, she exclaimed, "I lost me thong in there! I just lost me thong in there!" We laughed like kids as I stuck my arm in up to the elbow and retrieved it.

Anyway, we had passed the crisis and were headed downhill. Before sunup the doc and his son woke us up with a parting gift of coffee, then were on their way.

Sandra and I perched in the tent entrance, feeling on top of a world just being created. Fog was lifting so fast it looked like time-elapsed film. Rocks, timber, cliffs, and lakes spectacularly loomed up out of nowhere.

As a reward for living through the harsh side of Routeburn, we had received exclusive tickets to a private showing of a five-star movie exhibiting nature's most gorgeous colors and scenery—just for us.

We began walking and within thirty minutes were in glorious sunshine, our packs looking like portable clothes racks.

The journey continued to feel like a trek with the hobbits. First the terrain, then the adventure, next the gatherings and reunions with friends.

In a few hours we arrived at Lake Mackenzie, where we again met the doctor and his son, plus two other friends. And that night, at Lake Hawden, we saw them once more.

(Actually, the map names of lakes and other landmarks meant little, because of Sandra's delightful habit of christening or re-christening places with tags she deemed appropriate at the time: Thong Creek, Survival Summit, Sailor's Delight, and so on. These from a person who claimed to consciously **not** think, claimed she **couldn't** think, said she often had nothing, absolutely nothing, on her mind.)

The next day we hiked out to the road, all six of us, heading for Milford Sound. Because the doc had told acquaintances about us, we had to recount our fun little experience again and again, with rounds of ale, in front of the fire, amidst great camaraderie

I thought my times with Sandra had ended, but we met again the next night in Teanau, went dancing and drinking, and trekked back to the hostel about ten p.m. We found the whole gang up and lively, demanding another detailed account of our adventure on the mountain.

As in old fairy tales, strangers became friends, sharing adventures and stories they didn't completely understand, discussing the wonders of life and travel, laughing, toasting, listening and talking. Sandra and I had temporarily found the yellow brick road.

Still together the next morning, hitching north, we walked easily a long way, alone for the first time since Harris Saddle (Survival Summit). At Queenstown we said goodbye, and I never saw her again. We had a short, but not simple, parting of ways. Our eyes met for a moment, we held hands, smiled, and she turned away. I didn't get her off my mind for a long time.

The hobbit land of the Southern Alps
The obnoxious Kea birds would steal anything they could

The emergency hut at the summit of the Routeburn Track
The doc and beautiful next day weather // Harry Bryant's Lodge

3. ready, mates?

"...so I headed back to the ship"
—Bob Dylan's 115th Dream

February 3. The *Blue Orpheus* looked like a comforting nest, swaying gently in her slip. She looked like home.

I found good mail waiting for me, connecting me with old Berkeley friends, my folks, even Renee'. If anything in the world could help buck me up for the terrifying experiences ahead, those letters would.

DJ had the whole boat harbor under his spell, as though he had been there for months. Of course he sported a female companion, a plump half Maori woman, a good-natured soul, delighted by DJ's antics and cool confidence.

Steve and Lynn in the Auckland harbor

World-class boat builders and designers were dropping by regularly, discussing hull designs, rigging, sail cuts, new winch designs—and DJ obviously conversed on their level.

We all thought he had the means to build this seventy-two foot racing sloop everyone was talking about. It never happened, but you can't blame a guy for trying to live his dream. He loved yacht racing and had participated in some of the world's greatest races. It was natural for him to want to compete on a world-class level, in a world-class New Zealand built boat.

He received blueprints, designs, and advice from these men, worth countless dollars. Production on this mythical boat was to start "soon." Just a few loose ends to tie up back in the States. And he had just enough money to spend on the *Orpheus* to make his dream project believable.

He had had the *Orpheus* hull scraped and painted, the engine pulled and overhauled, the rigging checked meticulously. DJ had put her in really top shape for the journey home.

But she would be sailing without Mike and Corny, Dana, Tom, or DJ. All of them had made other plans—especially DJ, who would stay to hobnob with the boat experts for awhile, then fly back to Los Angeles to arrange charters for his sloop *Nam Sang*. He wanted me to obtain a captain's license after returning to the mainland, then run the big boat back to New Zealand.

He also intended to have me take the *Blue Orpheus* home with my own crew—all new, except for Jack.

I never for a moment considered saying no. Ye Gods— what an opportunity! What a responsibility and challenge. At the time, I overestimated the "opportunity" and underestimated the challenge and responsibilities.

DJ observed me as I readied the boat, wrote lists, and interviewed potential crew. Before I returned from the New Zealand countryside he had already chosen a replacement cook and her boyfriend—Carol and Rick. I chose Lynn, Steve, and Richard.

Lynn, a big New Zealander anxious for adventure, had the youth and strength to handle most of what was to come, even when things went completely beyond his expectations.

Steve, half Maori, was tall, lean, dark, with dancing but somehow disturbing blue eyes. His grandmother, a Maori witch doctor, had taught him much about the ocean and its mysteries.

Richard, as quick and natural a sailor as I have ever seen, had handled dinghies all his life. This kiwi hippie had a filthy mouth—but more than once I found myself admiring his eloquence.

When the Rolling Stones came to Auckland for an outdoor concert, Steve, Richard, and I attended. Our common interests as well as mutual support through later ordeals led us in time to become enduring friends.

I had some evenings alone with the *Orpheus*, leaning back in the cockpit, pondering the time to come. The beautiful southern sky displayed strange new constellations centered around the Southern Cross. The water lapped peacefully, so gently, at the hull. I still remember that secure sound, as I sipped wine, alone.

But my mind churned out worrisome facts and questions. I was about to take responsibility for a $65,000 boat and six other lives, across seven thousand miles of ocean. Had I gone crazy? Could I do it? Why did I want to? How would Jack be?

The nights sometimes proved worse than the evenings, when I would dream of death, or fires, or of rotting bodies coming to life, then burning.

When daylight ended the nightmares, new problems would arise. Jack, for instance. He argued with DJ that he had paid passage on the boat with DJ as captain, not some inexperienced kid. I couldn't really blame him for not wanting to sail with me in charge. DJ, however, was not giving money back. He very diplomatically dealt with Jack, convincing him that things would work out. Then DJ counseled **me** about what problems to expect from Jack and how to deal with them.

DJ applied reasonably effective strategy, but failed to deal with Jack's valid concerns—beyond jealousy. And I could only say I wanted to work with Jack, pretending we were still friends. Now, in retrospect, I see the utter folly of starting a trip under such conditions, trying to ignore potentially explosive chemistry.

When Tom came back on the boat for a few days, he acted worse than before. I remember him screaming in the ice cream parlor because he got two scoops instead of one. Crazy ranting and raving. I thought he finally had come to hate me for taking the boat—but I had no time or understanding of how to repair our relationship.

DJ expertly mixed work and play. In the midst of running a seemingly unending list of errands, and rounding up mountains of supplies, DJ could find a strategic time for a party. He introduced me to Diane, a friend of his Maori lady. We had fun together; she helped us, and later joined our bon voyage party. She must have believed I would be back—but so did I, then.

February 20. Just before departure on a voyage across the ocean, the excitement escalates into mass confusion, everybody rushing to get last minute jobs done. At that point, trying to monitor everything and comprehend the reality of leaving, I could hardly think—but watched Richard and Steve taping chafe points on the mast and spreaders, Jack tracking down an electrical problem, Carol stowing groceries in the galley, Rick gophering other last minute supplies. Everyone seemed to move at double speed.

DJ was off rounding up customs. He showed up about five p.m. with Diane and a case of beer. Dana and Tom came by shortly afterwards with another case. In the midst of goodbyes and talk of islands to come, we were still getting shipshape. DJ took the helm for the trip across the harbor to Queen's Wharf and Customs, after hanking the jib himself. I sat back, drinking kiwi beer, still bracing myself for difficulties ahead. If I could have fully anticipated them then, I might have jumped overboard.

At the wharf, food and champagne appeared. DJ spent a couple of minutes alone with me, giving me the okay, letting me know he understood what I was going through, forming a bond between us that still exists to this day.

As we left the dock, he had his jovial face back on. I can still see him standing there, yelling at us.

"Have fun, just don't put her up on a reef!"

I haven't been back to New Zealand. The *Nam Sang*, DJ's big sloop that I was supposed to skipper out of Los Angeles, limped into port in Auckland without me or a mast, about six months later. DJ had it chartered out bareboat—sans skipper—to fourteen rank amateurs who had to motor her six hundred miles after abusing and dismasting her.

Before that they had found Hawaii by following jet contrails.

Nam Sang had a controversial existence in New Zealand. DJ tells that story very well in the sequel *Stealing Nam Sang.*

In New Zealand I had encountered typically honest people in an honest culture. Thankful for the joy of knowing their country, I only hope it stays **non**-American. Nobody I know of would like the label of "**un**-American" or "**anti**-American, but moving out into the world far enough to see how many attractive **non**-American people and things there are—can change a person's perspectives. On my South Pacific trip I even found myself some-times looking back towards where I came from and asking, "Where are we going with this 'American' label, anyway? The United States is only a small part of the Americas; what exclusive pretensions do we have to the name of two entire continents? If we call ourselves Americans, what about everybody else in North, Central, and South America? What do they get to call themselves?

Part 3: Homeward Bound

1. warnings

"DECEMBER" (PART 1)

Fourteen days ago, the sun lost
His footing and fell in a drainage
Ditch. I can show you the place—
A stubble field near Schoolcraft. Today
Sleet peppers him from above and cornstalks
And marsh grass give him a cold
Finger from below. He might as well
Roll up in the bullrushes
And wait it out.

This morning a hawk
Flew low behind the house,
His hooks out, dragging the dark air,
Hunting the right life for himself.

—Conrad Hilberry, *Rust*

We sailed right smack into the son of a bitch

We sailed right smack into the son of a bitch.

Our crises began unthreateningly, about two days out; we encountered squally, gray weather, with winds of about force 4 to 5, 15 to 20 knots. I figured we'd have a couple of days of it, from the size of the low pressure ridge DJ had nonchalantly told me of before we cast off. I bitterly wished later that I'd looked at the weather pictures myself before sailing off. Probably, though, it did the unpredicted on its own, with no warning even to the experts.

Years later I learned that this vast piece of water is considered by many to be one of the five most dangerous in the world, primarily because of the 1,100 mile expanse without protection of any land. It is an area of lost lives and sailboats.

If we had known how bad it was going to get, we would have turned around before it peaked. "It," a tropical cyclone that came in on us from the northwest, developed out of a simple low pressure trough. Years before, during his circumnavigation, Chichester (the green flash observer) had taken a pounding from a storm that birthed in the same vicinity as ours. Combined with what he called a freak wave, it capsized him. Though he had been sailing in a different ocean—the Tasman, which has a reputation for treachery—I get a little comforted that even he was taken by surprise, shortly after leaving Sydney.

Days four and five exposed us to rougher weather, for a longer time, than any of us had ever before experienced. A steady force 6, 27 knots, showed no sign of a let-up.

To compound the problems, new, unexplainable electrical glitches began bothering us. First the bow running lights failed, next the bilge pumps shorted. The whole generator system seemed off, overcharging the batteries according to the gauges. I struggled with the malfunctions by myself, without success. Though Jack, even while sick, might have been able to fix things, he showed no inclination at all to help.

Driven by frustration and new worries about the weather, I switched from electricity textbooks to Bowditch on weather sailing. I hoped his comparison of typhoons and South Pacific hurricanes might help me figure out what we were getting into.

Like all other cyclonic storms of the Northern Hemisphere, the winds of the typhoon are directed counterclockwise around, and incline toward a center of low barometric pressure. On the contrary, the winds of the hurricanes of the South Pacific are directed clockwise around the center and more or less inward…the diameter of the wind system of the tropical cyclone may be as little as 20 or 30 miles, or as great as 300 to 500 miles, or even more…There is a pronounced gustiness of wind, even at the outer margins of the storm area; nearer the center the more violent winds are felt in very heavy squalls…

Since our worst stuff was coming in as huge squalls, not steadily as I would have expected, Bowditch's description fit our situation all too well. The author also spoke of barometer readings:

Barometric pressure at the center of some tropical cyclones is not as low as 29 inches, but it is usually lower in well-developed storms, and in exceptional

*cases falls below 28 or even to 27…The lowest reading
of record, 26.19 inches, was taken aboard a ship in
a typhoon east of Luzon in 1927…During the active
season of tropical cyclones, an unexpected fall of the
barometer of a tenth of an inch or more in 3 hours or
less, is nearly always an indication of the approach of
a cyclone.*

Those words added to my eerie conviction that we
faced some very heavy weather. Our barometer had dropped
according to the expected pattern. So what was I supposed to
do next? Bowditch's advice didn't help me very much.

*The best action to take in the event of a cyclonic storm
is to clear the storm area, or run for the navigable
semicircle and avoid the center of the storm as much
as possible…*

Which way would that be? On the basis of pilot charts
plotting other storms and their wind direction, I spent
confused hours trying to project the storm's movement and
our location in relation to its center—a guessing game that
ended in total frustration. We were holding our starboard
tack, and I had had enough sun to take good position fixes;
but which way should we go to reduce the beating we were
taking?

2. stern realities

The weather and constant **pounding and noise**
had begun telling on **us all.**

Richard and Steve—good friends-mates, in New
Zealand lingo—would still spend time in the cockpit together,
sometimes, when one of them was on watch. But our heavy
weather tended to isolate the others. As waves broke over the
Orpheus with increased regularity, the hatches had to stay
latched to keep the cabin dry. Life on board centered below
decks, in the bunks. The air got so stuffy, though (worsened
by widespread seasickness), that we occasionally had to risk
some flooding. Those ventilation periods inevitably ended
abruptly, with cursing, as a victim slammed the hatch shut
and began salvaging what dry items he could.

Richard does his galley magic

By the fourth day out, nearly everyone had been sick. The afflicted person would wait until the very last moment, then stumble crazily through the cabin and outside into the cockpit. Carol almost fell overboard when a wave hit as she hung over the downwind gunwale. After that scare, when the bigger waves hit she began letting out high-pitched, unnerving little shrieks.

We had double-reefed the mainsail, reducing its size considerably, and were using our smallest jib most of the time, dropping it at night and other times when the wind became overpowering. When the seas reached twenty-five feet, the *Orpheus* would pound heavily. To help slow us down and gain steerability I trailed two long ropes (warp lines) off the stern.

Even though we hadn't a dependable clue as to the storm center location, we thought we had chosen a sensible course, with the wind off the starboard beam. We were surfing the waves off the stern. Having fallen off the wind we were getting pushed north, of course, but doing our best to keep the boat in one piece.

The sense that we could hardly cope with weather any worse than we were getting, plus the fear that we might be drifting toward an extremely dangerous storm center made me decide, finally, on day seven, that the time had come to use the ham radio. DJ had operated it only a few times before, just enough for me to learn the preliminaries. I knew the call sign—HC0RJMM2 (translated "Henry Charlie Zero Romeo Juliet Mickey Mouse Two"). I knew how to raise the antenna off the fore and backstays with the staysail halyard, and knew how to warm up and tune the radio.

I went through the procedures, and the damn thing

refused to work. Since our leaving Auckland, it seemed that every blasted thing we tried had gone wrong! I felt an urgent need to fight the radio into submission.

I doggedly began replacing tubes with spares we had on board. After several hours I had come close to despairing when, suddenly, the device lit up, rattled with static, then squawked into life.

By even greater luck we contacted a ham named Art on a Coast Guard ice cutter in Antarctica. This man could share a treasure greater than gold—access to satellite weather photos for our area! My first visible—or at least audible— success as a skipper!

We arranged for a daily five p.m. rendezvous. The invaluable weather information showed, amazingly, that we had been doing about as well as could be expected. The center of the storm, which Art verified as cyclonic, lay northwest of us. We got daily updates on it and our position relative to it.

Art's transmissions comforted us more than words can convey. His daily radio conversations put us in touch with human civilization. They took place just before dark, the dreariest time of day. They became the center of our existence. They held our morale together. They kept us sane.

By the end of the first few days in the storm, we made some other contacts around the fringe to help us communicate with Art: Fred in Fiji, 3DQFM, Steve in California, WA61VN, and Barry in Rarotonga, our immediate destination. After very efficiently deducing who had the best contact with us, they would relay for Art and me when we couldn't talk directly with each other. We always heard them talking about us when we tuned the radio in.

The voices across the water gave us the kind of

reassurance that aviators know well, talking to Air Traffic Control, a person in a dark windowless room, miles away, safe and dry, who can make them feel that they just might make it after all, in spite of storms and emergencies.

Even with the giant consolation of radio, though, people and things were falling apart on board the *Orpheus*. We had to relieve Rick from watches, on account of sickness. I took on his helm duty. The goddam engine quit again, because of another fuel line leak. After lying belly deep in bilge water for several hours, skinning my knuckles as usual, I had it fixed. The seas often loomed thirty feet. We surfed on most of them, but inevitably some broke over us, crazily jolting the boat into making strange groans. The wind never ended; its sounds varied, though, from awesome bellows to high-pitched shrieks. The halyards clanked against the mast as we sank into a wave bottom, then all the rigging would creak and strain as the *Orpheus* crested.

We continued evening and morning inspections of the boat, but with two crew members instead of one. A break of crucial equipment, especially at night, could leave us in desperate trouble. We studied every chafe point and rigging connection—twice as often as usual. About halfway through the storm, the *Orpheus* began to leak.

Jack and I both had close calls on the bow, changing sails at night. Since we had no real storm jib, but needed something up there for balance, we had to use a bigger sail and just drop it when it got too rough. Jack went forward without a harness and slipped across the deck to the lee side when a wave hit him. Later, my harness slipped loose— evidently I didn't get it hooked properly in the dark—and after a huge wave slammed us I wound up on my back, legs overboard and in the water, holding onto the weak stanchion lines. Going overboard in those conditions would have been fatal. Luckily, wildly, we each managed to catch ourselves.

Carol could no longer cook. Lyn and Steve usually managed to put something together for us. Nothing ever affected their appetites, even when they were sick. They had the digestive apparatus of a pair of goats. Richard, the poor bugger, could not eat for a week.

Our situation gave us absolutely nothing to smile about, and yet, occasionally, you would see brief grins in appreciation of Richard's profanity. It so eloquently, so inventively, helped to relieve our frustration.

I once read the famous curse of Bishop Ernulphus, which takes the space of two pages or more to excommunicate and damn some poor sinner to eternal perdition and torture. It invokes the heavenly powers—saints, angels, archangels, and whatever. It mentions every bodily function, every moment of the day. It lays down a fairly complete inventory of afflictions, wishing them all on the named victim.

There was world-class swearing that has never been topped, to my knowledge, but Richard was not altogether out of Ernulphus's league. In fact, as we witnessed him mature and grow in his ability to express disapproval of wind and weather, boat smells, sail and wave behavior, cookery, and so on, I occasionally wondered if we didn't have on board the great Bishop himself, reincarnated.

The storm worsened continually. After five days of seeing it grow stronger and us grow weaker, we were just hanging on, struggling for basic survival. And we weren't halfway through it. Our wind meter topped at 55 knots and stayed pegged a lot of the time.

I had to fight off waves of nauseating panic. What if the engine quit again? What if I couldn't get the s.o.b. going? No battery power, no lights, no radio, no freezer, no bilge pumps. What if this storm gets worse? What if we're lost? (I was confused about the date line, which would make a difference in our position of about ten miles). What if the boat starts leaking worse, or breaks, or someone falls overboard…?

Well, as things turned out in the long run, at least the boat didn't really break.

As my fears came to look more and more like real possibilities that might confront us, I had to think about the capacities of the crew and me to survive a catastrophe. What resources did ordinary people like us have to withstand disasters? We measured up as more than rank amateurs, but far less than the many who have sailed the Horn, solo or crew, or ventured around the world (recently, at least, in high-tech equipment that wasn't stopping or shorting out or breaking down).

Four of us had become average ocean sailors, with a few thousand miles behind us. Steve, in fact, had survived a tropical cyclone (hurricane, in the southern hemisphere) at sea near Fiji.

But every one of us was afraid at one time or another during the following week. We estimated the wind's steady peak at force ten, which translates to fifty-five to sixty-three knots per hour. Steve thought that at one point it reached hurricane force for thirty minutes or so.

Wave height was difficult to judge and impossible to show in photographs. The two-dimensional limit just flattened out waves; from the trough, though, looking up at them, you felt like a gopher in the Grand Canyon. Almost no sky was visible. They appeared higher than the mast, dwarfing the boat, and about to completely submerge us as they crested. But we would magically ride up the side, usually taking on only part of the crest. Then, like climbing a mountain, we would get a momentary glimpse of the world, all wet as it was. At least things looked survivable from the crests. We would be headed back down in a hole, but had been reassured that the top was still there, that there was an escape from the bottom. Who knows how high the waves really were, but probably no more than thirty-five feet at the worst.

Six days out, I found the bilges almost full and investigated. When I went to the forward cabin and emptied the main hatch under the double bunk, the sight was mesmerizing. As the *Orpheus* plunged from one wave to the next, the bow became airborne, and I could see light through the translucent sandwich fiberglass construction. She gave a tremendous shudder every time she dove back into the ocean, and I could see it reverberating back through the rest of the hull.

At first it stopped my breathing, when I thought the hull was coming apart. I quickly realized the fiberglass was solid, though, and then an odd fascination took over and I must have been glued there for ten minutes, watching the ocean and rigging above work the hull. It twisted, pounded, and hammered the boat from every angle with deafening crashes. I eventually left the bow with more faith than ever in the *Orpheus'* basic construction.

She was leaking mainly through the chainplates because of the stress on the mast rigging, and also a little through the through-hull fittings. Everbody's bunk was wet near the chainplates. Most of our clothing was wet, too, and the main hatches leaked even when tightly latched.

* * *

New Zealand to Rarotonga was 1,600 nautical miles, great circle route. On February 28, eight days out, I had fixed us at 25° 48' S, 169°, 00' W. We had been making sixty to one hundred-sixty miles every twenty-four hours. And we had gone two days without enough sun for a good fix.

Close to desperation as we were, all of us except Rick and Carol tried to maintain the appearance of sanity and "calm." Carol cried a lot, sometimes in a loud wail. We could hear her in the forward cabin. Rick's eyes became wild and darting, unable to focus on anyone. He muttered to himself. If he thought us all crazy for being there, he probably had that right. But at least we were generally "all there," which was more, before long, than you could say for him.

Nothing I could do would help them. We needed a psychiatrist for that (or else a couple of straitjackets, maybe). I had my hands full with taking over Rick's helm duties, navigating, keeping a log, doing diesel maintenance (a job I soon would be forced to abandon), operating the radio, running the boat, and trying to preserve my sanity. More than once I wondered why in hell I had listened to DJ. To handle his 40 foot boat in the middle of the ocean in a full blown gale like this one, to take responsibility for six other lives and tens of thousands of dollars worth of equipment— he didn't need a 22-year-old like me. He needed a Captain Ahab, or a Captain Bligh—or maybe the Ancient Mariner himself, or maybe Noah.

Aside from our wild-eyed couple, though, the *Orpheus* had a spunky crew—sailors who wanted to sail, who scorned the options of sea anchors or going bare poles (without any sails). Without some sail up we felt helpless and out of control.

The helm demanded constant, expert attention. To broach on one of the huge waves—move into it sideways—meant a very good chance of swamping or capsizing our boat. The helmsman had to keep the stern to the wave as we surfed down the front side at up to ten or twelve knots, then crawl back up the back side, sometimes having to angle at the bottom to keep the bow from digging into the trough, all the while minding the wind to at least keep it on the right side of the boat.

The helmsmen allowed the boat to jibe a few times, and strained the rigging somewhat, but those accidental turns had mostly happened at the bottom of a wave where the wind wasn't quite as strong. The boomvang consistently held. (The vang was a line off the boom to a downwind cleat to prevent it from slamming over in the event of back-winding the mainsail.)

Two hours of steering, facing an awesome outside world, would leave a helmsman bone tired. I respected thankfully the jobs Steve, Richard, Lyn, and Jack were doing. All four of them, strong, stoic, good helmsmen, quietly handled their share. I didn't worry about them giving up or doing the wrong thing. But I wouldn't have put Rick at the helm at that point even if he had volunteered. Even if he had paid. On the other hand, for a ticklish situation at night when you could hardly see the waves, Richard and Steve had the best touch.

A sailor notices the way the sea changes colors to match a thousand different moods, and seems to worship sunshine. On bright days even the biggest waves look tamer and bluer. But in the overcast, with the wind blowing the tops off the crests, the sea turns battleship grey, with a mood to match—unfortunately, a mood contagious to people.

We hadn't seen enough of the sun for three days to get a decent fix. Handling the sextant required two men and the most extreme care. Saltwater alone would corrode and insult the beautiful instrument, but we could get by with one slightly damaged by sea water. If we dropped it, though, and ruined its accuracy, we would not know where we were—ignorance, in that case, not being "bliss," but potential destruction.

To get topside with the sextant, I would take it out of its case and hand it to someone sitting solidly on the cockpit ladder. Then I would slide past him up to the cockpit, where he would pass it back to me. Then he would climb up by the mast, where I would come for the shot after handing the sextant over. The timekeeper also helped hold me steady and watched for waves coming overboard while I attempted to get a shot.

Our radio contacts continued, even though at times I could send only estimates of our position. Those sessions helped salvage our morale after a terrible day. We all crouched around to listen, trying to convince ourselves that we were not the only human beings left on earth or sea. But though those sessions helped us keep going, we all felt beat to death, and getting weaker.

3. near catastrophe

On March 1, our ninth day out of Auckland, our seventh in various facets of the storm, the whole crew reached the bottom of its biorhythm scale, while facing the top of the gale.

At two a.m., during the very worst blow, the clue point in the mainsail gave way, sending a twenty-five inch tear across the face of the sail before we could get it down. We tied the sail around the boom, transferred to diesel power, and returned to our bunks. I lay in my bunk, hoping the sail was repairable, thinking what a tough "seamstress" job for someone.

Diesel power gave us a different ride. The prop often cleared the water as the boat surfed down a wave, then the prop would catch and help push us up the back side. Without sails we rocked and pitched more violently, but that uncomfortable motion didn't last long enough to concern us. Two hours later, at four a.m., we were all up fighting for our lives.

The engine had caught fire.

Jack was on watch, and first noticed the instrument lights go dim. About the same time I came to, smelling smoke. I opened the engine hatch and was forced back by billowing smoke. I yelled to wake everyone up and evacuated them to the cockpit, with orders to ready the life raft.

Keeping low to avoid the smoke, I activated the fire extinguisher on the engine. It still burned.

I had to reach the main electric power switches, up above the engine hatch. I poked my upper body up through the thickest smoke to reach in and cut the power. The plastic switches came apart in my hand, melted. Jack crawled down through the cockpit hatches to disconnect the batteries while the crew handed me buckets of water to throw on the flames. Though nauseated, having inhaled a lot of smoke, I doused the fire. The crew pulled me out to fresh air. I felt too weak to climb the ladder.

We sat back in the cockpit, letting the smoke clear, allowing our adrenaline to subside. All of us were visualizing the scene if we had popped the life raft CO_2 charge, abandoned the *Blue Orpheus*, and gone down, in the dark, into that wild water.

One by one we retreated to our bunks. I lay awake, my mind an empty waste. I suddenly didn't dare look in a mirror. I felt so old—ancient, but without even an average man's wisdom, much less a Methuselah's. And I felt so tired. I doubted my capacity to handle anything more. First the storm, then no sun to navigate by, then blown out sails, now a fire. What dire next ordeal was waiting for us? Was God conspiring against us with the ghost of Captain Bligh, who navigated and sailed a life raft across the Pacific?

I felt just as tired when we evaluated the mess in the daylight. White fire retardant chemical everywhere, equipment scattered, torn sails lashed down on deck, an exhausted, seasick crew stumbling around on their way out to upchuck. The seas feeling wilder than ever as we tossed around, dead in the water.

Richard set to mending the mainsail. He had lots of previous experience, sewing colored patches over colored patches on every pair of Levis he owned. Day ten, after eight days of stormy weather, the seas mercifully seemed to be abating.

As Jack and I investigated the fire, we discovered that because the starter switch had not been springing back, the starter had heated up and shorted out. That switch problem explained other earlier electric glitches and shorts. Both of the 3/8-inch starter solenoid wires had burned completely through.

Then we found, with horror, a fuel line almost melted. If it hadn't stayed intact, if raw diesel fuel had fed the flame...

Difficult as it was to believe, we could have been unluckier. A lot unluckier.

4. goodbye, world!

**We cleaned up as best we could under the
circumstances, and wired the ham radio
directly to the batteries for limited
transmitting power. We had no way now
to start the engine or charge the batteries.**

Our radio contact that evening terrifically boosted morale—though Art, appalled at our story, hardly knew what to say. Without friendly voices like his from the outside we could have just given up in despair, confined to our small, miserable world. Some of us on the *Orpheus*, natural loners, probably appreciated more than once the absence of companions; but this latest shipboard trauma turned us

More sail mending

around for the time being, anyway, made us grateful for the human race occupying a wide world beyond ours. Our occasional radio contacts sent shivers down my spine.

When you are isolated long enough, as we had been, time loses its perspective. An hour can seem like a day, a week like a lifetime. The daily events necessary for existence assume such absorbing importance that the rest of the world fades into unreality, like a long-ago dream. Talking to the outside world woke us up, brought us back, like a slap in the face.

A book we happened to have on board, *The Strange Last Voyage of Donald Crowhurst,* offered frightening evidence of the impact of isolation. It recorded the tragedy of a man who had entered the solo round-the-world sailing race. He went insane and eventually jumped overboard. Later, his empty boat was found with the logs intact showing the strange path he took from normalcy to insanity and death.

With Richard's substantial-looking mainsail patch, at least we were sailing again, and could so report. We were also getting sunshine, enough for a good position fix. But the loss of bilge pumps worried us. We couldn't use the electric ones, and broke the manual one. After that, we could only keep buckets handy, feeling crippled, not to mention vulnerable.

We knew that, with no recharging capability, our battery could give us only limited radio communications. After two days, we had our last talk with Art, Barry, Fred, and Steve. As we tuned up we heard them talking back and forth about our misfortunes. One of them said, "Man, those guys must be hard as nails." What a great compliment, especially coming at a time when the "nails" felt beaten, bent, and rusted! Fred told the others Fiji had a thousand-man search and rescue team standing by.

I broke in, said hi, gave our position, told them the weather finally seemed to be improving, we were safe and doing fine. A few minutes later the batteries lost power. Our communication with the outside world ended.

5. the influence of grandparents

**Sometime the next night, perhaps early in
the morning, something similar to a dream,
but clearer and closer to consciousness,
closer to reality, came to me: a re-enactment
of an event of many years past.**

As a young boy I had been with my family at a summer cottage near an inland Michigan lake. My grandfather, Joe Williams, then an old man, had come all the way from California to visit—the only time he ever did.

My dad wanted to rent a boat and take Grandpa out. Or rather, have him take us out. Though everyone thought Dad was crazy, he persisted.

"More than fifty years ago my father sailed professionally, made his living as a fisherman, more than fifty years ago. Now I'm over forty, he's never had me out in a boat, and this is the chance I've waited years for. If he's game, I am—and I guarantee the kids will be safe."

Grandpa was old, in rather poor health, and hadn't sailed for decades. Because of threatening weather and a whippy wind, the marina people had planned to close for the day. Dad convinced them, though, they shouldn't pass up a profitable rental, and their Lido would never be in more competent hands.

I remember Grandpa just kind of shuffling along, not saying much of anything. Dad knew less about sailing than I did—I had been taking lessons in summer camp. But he showed absolutely unshakeable confidence in the old man.

Like eager little puppies, Dad and I clumsily followed Grandpa's directions. He didn't "order" us, just simply stated things we could do. After we left the dock and got sailing, I saw Grandpa in an unforgettable but totally natural pose— white hair blowing, his small grey and white mustache a distinctive feature in a dark, weather-beaten face. I especially noticed the blue grey eyes, shadowed by huge grey eyebrows, watering in the wind, looking up at the sails and out to the water.

He had us play with the sails, trimming and setting them until he sat comfortably at the tiller, sometimes holding it with just a finger or two, and sometimes just sitting there with his hands folded together—in white capped water and a fifteen knot breeze! (Later, he explained to me that, as a fisherman, he often needed both hands free to haul nets or do other emergency chores. In a race, a sailor would use altogether different methods.)

I remember best, though, the moment on the lake when, in his romantic (to me) Cornish accent he said,

"See, Dickie, there's no reason to fight her. Just trim her out properly. Most boys try to run too much sail."

Spellbound, my father and I looked at each other as Grandpa sat perfectly relaxed, perfectly at home, as though more than fifty years had just been erased, and he was a twenty-year-old again, fishing off the Isle of Wight.

I loved it when he called me Dickie. And I hated it when anybody else did.

I never got to know my grandfather well. In fact we had a falling out later, during my late teens. When my long hair bothered him, he had the nerve to say so—to a smart, sophisticated college kid! (Actually, he sort of nagged me about the hair, every chance he got.) And then he died, before we ever found something better to talk about. I regret that now more than I used to.

Anyhow, waking up, I felt I had received not just a beautiful vision, not just a gift from the only grandfather I had known—no, somehow, he had found a way to do even more, to pass along my inheritance from him. I saw the episode in a new light, with a new lesson.

I returned to consciousness refreshed, confident, off the bottom bilges where I had been wallowing for days. We were going to make it.

* * *

March 4: 21° 30' S, 164° 40' W. Steve went out, stood in the wind, and spoke a Maori chant his grandmother had taught him. He wouldn't say anything about what it was or meant, but within thirty minutes the blow began letting up. We didn't dare talk about it. (I wished to hell he had done it ten days earlier.)

Reveling in lots of sunshine, we shifted to a port tack, back on course. The gale was pooping out. The seas still thrashed around, crazy and upset, but smaller. The wind had dropped to twenty-five knots. And I was about as impressed with Steve's grandmother as I was with my grandfather. She hadn't stopped whispering Maori secrets to him, either, as I soon learned.

Several of us were out on deck enjoying the sun and fresh air that afternoon, with Jack at the helm. Suddenly, out of nowhere, a wild gust almost laid us down. When it hit we had been running right along with a small jib and one reef in the main.

The mainsheet jammed on a winch as we tried to ease it. Jack was hanging on to the wheel with all his might. We were taking water in the cockpit by the time Richard could drop the main halyard. The attack lasted maybe thirty seconds, and left us shaken and dazed. A real slam dunk, gone as suddenly as it had come. It was as though the storm had taken us in its teeth, and given us a final shake to teach us respect.

"What in the hell **was** that?" somebody asked to no one in particular. We all just looked at each other, unsmiling. No one answered. **Twice** this happened, in two days? The first time came just after the storm had hinted it might ease up on us a bit; Jack had been at the helm then, too. Jack also had been helmsman when the fire started.

That evening, the first one pleasant enough to spend outside, Steve and Richard talked to me. They seriously believed Jack had fallen under a Maori curse that had been jinxing the *Orpheus*. During his travels in New Zealand, Jack had confessed to Steve, he had slept in a Maori graveyard, in spite of being warned not to. Jack had evidently been caught in a rainstorm, and the graveyard afforded some shelter.

"That is a curse," Steve said, "and we have been paying for it."

Now the moon is almost hidden
the stars are beginning to hide
the fortune-telling lady
has even taken all her things inside.

— *Bob Dylan, "Desolation Row"*

What the hell could I do about it, even if he had got himself jinxed? I owed Jack. He had done his share very well, too, up to this point, and I had been thankful for his strength and engineering expertise. Besides, where would we find a whale to stow Jack/Jonah away in? I understood Steve's and Richard's feelings, though—and wondered, later, if Steve **hadn't** got some authentic messages from Grandma.

6. a boat divided

Things kept happening to keep us from relaxing.

The next day, as the weather warmed, a scuba tank pressure relief valve opened. It had been stored under Rick's and Carol's forward bunk. When it suddenly produced a loud pop and hiss, Rick and Carol shot out of their cabin like rockets, their eyes wide with terror. They thought a hole had been blown in the hull. The looks on their faces made us laugh, but their mental state was anything but funny in fact; they had just "gone over the edge."

With the release of that scuba air out flooded fear, panic, and hatred that had built up inside Rick and Carol during the storm. They had miseries, I knew, like the rest of us. But I hadn't picked up on anything more serious than that. Carol had been tossed across the galley a few times by sudden boat motion, and I had half-noticed how often she would burst into tears. But I had assumed she would recover, like the rest of us, with the end of the storm and a little sunshine. For her greater security, I had given her my bunk on the more secure, lee side and had not perceived her emotional needs to be greater than anyone else's.

The rest of us were relieving our tensions by becoming rope-a-dope, silly, like teenagers after an all night party. We fought over biscuits, good naturedly, teasing and giggling. But Rick and Carol would not join in, talk, or associate with us.

After the tank popped, with Carol screaming hysterically, Rick just came unglued, howling at me about the awful danger of keeping those tanks aboard. People were going to get killed. Explanation of the safety valve and its operation did nothing for him.

After that incident Rick and Carol avoided the rest of us, making life on board the small boat even more uncomfortable. The others just ignored them, too, probably the best thing to do at the time. I underestimated the seriousness of the problem in two ways: I didn't realize how nearly pathological they both had become; and I didn't suspect them of having a gun.

I continued Rick's watches; he claimed illness. We were on double watches at night so one man could hold a flashlight on the compass.

I was fighting off what was, to me, a new kind of fear. I had experienced the sudden, quick terror known to aviators. When an engine suddenly quits, or another airplane appears in your windscreen for a split second, adrenaline flows so quickly through your veins that it momentarily paralyzes like a seizure—for an instant every muscle involuntarily grows rigid. But the emotion doesn't last for more than a second or two. If it did there could be no reaction to the problem. And the problem, no matter how serious, lasts only briefly. Aircraft can't stay airborne more than a few hours, so the fear can't persist longer than that.

Sailing was different. The fear could last for days. It could make you feel old and more tired than you could have imagined. Sometimes it made you want to cry. Time stood still.

We had been at sea two weeks, in the teeth of the storm for about six days, and around the fringes of it for probably nine days.

7. intermission: gifts from home

"STOP ACTION"
(FOR BROWNIE GALLIGAN)

Slowly as in an underwater dance
the shortstop dips to take the ball
on a low hop, swings back his arm, balancing
without thought, all muscles intending
the diagonal to the first baseman's glove.

As the ball leaves his hand, the action stops-
and, watching, we feel a curious poignancy,
a catch in the throat. It is not this play
only. Whenever the sweet drive is stopped
and held, our breath wells up like the rush
of sadness or longing we sometimes feel
without remembering the cause of it.
The absolute moment gathers the surge
and muscle of the past, complete,
yet hurling itself forward-arrested
here between its birth and perishing.

—Conrad Hilberry

Grandpa's appearance in my dream came as a surprise.

I hadn't been thinking about him, but suddenly, there he was. Maybe the old man somehow arranged "transportation" to tell me hair is hair, bygones are bygones. Maybe he only wanted me to become a good man, strong enough to know when and how to be gentle. Or maybe he knew I needed consolation from a real sailor.

Anyway, he started something. I found myself thinking more often about the past, and one night I sort of "went home again," while lying on my bunk, trying to relax before my turn at the wheel. Maybe I needed a session with two favorite teachers. (During most of their lives both my parents had taught other people. My mother had credentials to handle anything from first grade through community college. My father taught in college.)

I'm not sure what they did to help me change in a few years from a timid toddler to a brash, rash sixth grader. I had ventured into life pretty apprehensively, I realized, never welcoming surprises.

The family still teases me about my fearful rejection of the whole state of Wyoming, when I was about four. On a visit to the old family homestead there, our car got mired down on a hilly, muddy bentonite road. Terrified that our vehicle wouldn't go where we wanted it to, I whined, "I don't like this stinkin' plyce!" (The family also still wonders where my crazy mixture of Cornish and Cockney came from—and so do I.)

Kindergarten confused and shocked me—and once, getting on the wrong bus nearly destroyed me. Something happened to turn around that fear of new adventures or challenges. What was it?

The answer might explain a triumphant episode that happened during my sixth-grade year, when shyness had been replaced by the ability—literally—to blow my own horn. Earlier my mother had pushed me into piano lessons, and when I began to take an interest in cornet, too (or instead!), she got me a beaten-up Pan American cornet when I was in fifth grade. My great coup with it came the following year, after I had first publicly embarrassed myself.

While a new school building was getting built, sixth through ninth grades went together. I joined the large, quite good band, consisting of mostly older juveniles. We marched at basketball games, and at one rehearsal I arrived with my horn case locked and no key. Mom brought the key down, and I proudly pulled out the Pan American, which I had just disassembled and completely cleaned. But I had put the valves in the wrong cylinders and couldn't blow a note. I sat in the bleachers fiddling with my instrument during the entire rehearsal, getting plenty of giggles and jeers from the older band members. I was stricken, and my older sister, who played flute, was downright mortified. Having established quite a reputation as a nerd, I sat in the third cornet section pretty much ignored by our leader, a young fellow fresh out of college, good but impatient and cool, definitely not a nerd.

This band director encouraged challenges. Once a week anyone could challenge anyone else for a higher seat. The two opponents would go into a side room and play selections as player #1 and player #2. Afterward, the other band members would choose the winner by vote.

One day, feeling cocky, I dared to challenge the first chair player, a popular kid who sat just below the solo trumpeter. Instead of playing against the guy next above me, about six seats below the first chair, I took on the person seven chairs up. We went into our little room.

After I had finished, and the first trumpet began, I could hear giggles outside. The band was hearing noises they thought came out of my Pan American. But the other fellow was screwing up, and I had played circles around him.

After an almost unanimous vote for player #1, the band director couldn't believe his ears when he learned I had won. My poor sister, who had to sit through the whole thing, stood up and cheered. (I've never asked her which one she had voted for.)

The best part came after school, walking home. Jenny McKenna, an eighth grader I had a crush on, caught up with me and told me what a great job I had done. I ecstatically traveled the rest of the way home on cloud nine.

Of course my parents rejoiced with me, especially my mother, who had helped me get started, and endured some pretty awful beginner's practice noises.

I began remembering other things about my mother. Good things about her. Besides teaching in between times, she had raised four children without much money, but a lot of hard work. A jumble of images came back to me—Mom, using a rubber scraper in a peanut butter jar to get the last glob. Mom, trying to "sleep in" a little bit on Saturday mornings. Mom, insisting on piano lessons for all of us. Mom, making me practice, pitting her determination against my strong preference for playing outside. Mom, giving us our first dog, when I was ten.

She made terrific sacrifices in order to obtain property

in Michigan where family roots were. Then she worked, and made us all work, to transform a shack into a summer cottage by the river—not just a home, but a homing center.

In spite of the resistance I must have had, family activities shoved me into new experiences. We traveled a lot—too much for me to get too comfortable in any one place. And my mother—disciplinarian, friend and helper, opener of doors, supporter of independence—kept pushing me, or helping me help myself, into wider worlds.

Maybe my folks took turns doing the "good cop/ bad cop" routine (according to that story-book procedure, after one policeman has been "mean" to a suspect, and got nowhere, the partner takes over and kindly, gently, extracts a confession!). My father opposed my having a gun, Mom took responsibility for my prudent handling of a single shot .22, and then Dad taught me how to handle it safely.

Three years earlier, my mother had gotten me a bow and arrow. She even helped me buy my first motorcycle. At the end of my sophomore year in high school Mother arranged to let me stay on a cousin's place for a wonderful summer of Wyoming ranch life, working with cattle, buffalo, sheep, and horses. It was there I first learned to drive, and got my first airplane ride, from my cousin.

Earlier, when I was a fifth-grader, my mother guided me into an early morning paper route, as an attempt to channel my growing independence into productive activities. That job gave my dog some new duties, too. We spent hours together, me on my bike, the red mutt running alongside. I would get up at five a.m., bike across town with my dog, pick up my papers at a corner newsstand, roll them, pack them in my saddlebags, and head out in the dark, in a trance-like state.

I put a few thousand miles on that bike, often in snow and cold, or rain. Sometimes I could get home in time to sleep thirty minutes or so before getting up for school. I often dreamed I had delivered all the papers to the wrong houses, or that I had suddenly forgotten where they were supposed to go, with no list to fall back on.

A paper route is supposed to build character. I'm not sure mine did. On some cold snowy mornings I would fake illness well enough to make my mother get up with one of my sisters to run the route with a car—or sled. I don't even remember feeling guilty about it. But the job required a lot of time alone with my own thoughts—useful training. I finally accepted, even enjoyed, that kind of solitude.

My dog and I formed a lasting bond, just the way the books describe it. Twelve years later he died—run over while he was sleeping near the edge of the road—a habit we had tried in vain to break him of. The news left me flooded with fond emotions as I remembered our times together, just the two of us.

One spring, when I was in high school, I qualified for a well-known international music camp in Michigan, not far from our cottage. (Our high school band director, a crusty Italian trumpet virtuoso, had taken me under his wing, and made me a reasonably competent first leader in my section. I'll always honor him for his gruff kindness and friendship.)

Without that high school training, I might not have qualified for the music camp—but, ironically, once I got there, I hated it. The people reminded me of my junior high schoolmates in a Chicago suburb: rich little primadonnas, fiercely competing. I had a poor instructor who did me more harm than good.

I hardly dared tell my folks how I felt. Mom was so proud of me, and tuition cost more than the folks could really spare. But I did benefit from exposure to the classical world of music, and I learned to sail there.

My senior year capped the relationship with my mother. I took honors English, comp and lit, with her as teacher. I made it tough on her at times, as she did for me, but we became very close. She was so youthful, so agreeable to us, so open to our thinking. All my friends loved her, and she was our senior class advisor.

* * *

At two a.m. Richard came below to wake me for my two hour watch. I had been dreaming, or something close to it. I rolled out of the quarter bunk, pulled on a wool sweater, Levis, and thongs, grabbed rain gear, took a drink of water, and pulled myself up the ladder and into the cockpit. I hung over the stern with an arm hooked around the backstay, relieving myself, while Richard quietly briefed me on weather, sails, and heading.

After we have traded places at the helm Richard takes a leak, jumps below to fill a bowl with rice pudd (Kiwi slang for pudding), and returns above to join me and wind down before bed.

I enjoy his comfortable company. We leave a lot unsaid, just taking things in together. In spite of a few squalls around, the night seems pleasant. For a change the cockpit offers good hospitality. After fifteen or twenty minutes of easy banter, Richard says goodnight and heads below. I'm alone now, and don't mind that, either.

Almost immediately I was drawn back in time again.

After reviewing once more my great sixth grade musical triumph, it surprised me to find myself thinking about the poor bugger I beat. He must have suffered quite a lot, losing out to a nerd. Had the intervening years taught me a little compassion? Well, maybe the years had also made me forget a precious idea: "You don't know it's impossible unless you try; why not try?"

I also thought briefly about my lack of conscience as a paper boy, after faking illness and making my mother and sister take over my job. Well, after all, I at least know now I should have felt twinges of guilt. My mother must have taught me something, after all.

* * *

I could see a squall up ahead that would soon cross our path, but it didn't look too big. I decided to try getting by with just luffing the main out a little, thinking,

"Geez, a pretty night, really, no moon, plenty dark, lots of stars out. And warm. Why put the slicker on? The fresh water will feel good. After daylight we might even go out of our way to hit the squall for fresh water showers and refreshment. Wind's coming up a bit, though."

I tied the wheel, and ran forward to drop the genoa until we were past the squall. No sense waking someone to help—this one's easy to handle.

* * *

During my college days, my father sort of took over where my mother left off. I remember very little of him during childhood, but thought of him as a serious scholar, fighting for an education between jobs pulling ice, driving a truck, running a jack hammer, doing shipping clerk and/or janitorial work, being timekeeper in a cherry cannery, waiting tables, inspecting parts in a chain factory, and overseeing avocado orchards. It took him three separate enrollments and eleven years to earn his B.A. degree. He finally finished his doctorate when I was in first grade.

He later confessed to me I had him pegged wrong as a serious scholar. I'd be closer to the mark thinking of him as an American "Lucky Jim"—a working class stiff who had invaded a world of higher education he didn't quite belong in, as a slightly frivolous, erratic teacher. Dad said he was at best a "hands on" thinker who mistrusted any ideas that lacked some tangible connections, and who found comfort escaping from the classroom into the workshop.

I remember ice skating with him a couple of times, on the pond behind the old farmhouse we had rented in upstate New York. And all of us trudging out through the snowy woods to get a Christmas tree one year.

He spanked me a few times, but his worst torture was to sit and talk to his unruly children, seemingly for hours on end. If he was trying to get inside our heads, I must have frustrated him, because I would not respond. During the "little" chats with me, he wasted a lot of breath, just talking to thin air. Most of the time my mind had escaped to far off places, even alien planets. But he would continue to probe. What he did, I realized eventually, was let me inside his head—but it took me a while to understand and accept that.

As we drove together from Illinois to Missouri, when I was fourteen, we had a rare (at that time) long communication, talking of life. We even talked of Beowulf (who became suddenly transformed from a brutish "bee wolf"—a "bear" of a man—into a polished state ruler). I realize now, some of my father's dreams for me sneaked into the conversation.

I think that was the last intimate talk we had for about six years. But we worked together some, during that interval. He said that even though I was learning to survive by my wits in a hostile world, I also ought to be able to support myself with my hands if necessary. So Dad passed along a "profession" he had taught himself—tuning and repairing pianos.

He got an old junker for me that someone was going to haul to the dump. I learned enough to earn college money, but constantly had to fight boredom to learn to tune a piano. And it took me a long time to get good at it.

I used to consider myself a disappointment to my father. I took nothing seriously. I was not letting my schooling interfere with my education, as the saying goes. (I didn't in college, either.) I rarely studied, cruised Main Street whenever I could. I liked girls. Sometimes I wondered what he thought, watching me have fun, maybe remembering his high school days during the depression, when he saw gangs of carefree kids like me from the inside of the grocery store where he had to work.

As dean of a college in Missouri, he still had to work pretty long hours. He had a large study in our house, with bookshelves going all the way up to the nine foot ceiling—all full. A few times, when I came home about one in the morning, he would be in there—and back again by five. (I didn't get up myself—just heard about him from the family.) He got to very few of my music and drama performances.

But he did speak at a high school graduation one year. I felt extremely proud of him, and also of myself for being his son.

Maybe I make my father sound terrible—a distant person whose career made him ignore his family. That's not true. If we pretended to ignore one another, we really had a secret admiration society. He later made me understand how he felt about me during those high school years. He envied my carefree times, true, but hadn't minded that I refused to take school seriously. He had done the same at my age, rejecting lessons that didn't make sense. He quoted Thoreau: *"In wildness is the hope of civilization."* Seems Dad even took pride in my wildness!

* * *

The storm touched us, then went its way. The ideal squall: warm, short, sweet, just a nice diversion. I moved back to the bow to untie and raise the genoa. After a bit of re-trimming I could check the compass, then sit back to relax.

A tremendous display of meteorites appeared before long, more than one a minute, some visible five or more seconds. Mom couldn't—or shouldn't—worry about me on a night like this.

* * *

I read that some famous man once said,
When I was fourteen, I thought my father an idiot.
But by the time I turned twenty-one, I was amazed
at how much the old man had learned in seven years.

That's about what it took for me, too. We began communicating on a common wavelength during my junior year at Berkeley. By then Dad was working with a new experimental college in southern California. During those years the war and campus riots were tearing the country apart, fathers and sons at odds everywhere; funny, but that's the time we became close.

He was so objective. So open, with occasionally unexpected input, with so much love. We hugged each other. I read his writing, listened to his speaking, able to appreciate them for the first time, wondering, where has this guy been? I came to respect and admire him as I had never respected or admired anyone before. And he treated me like a man. It was better than having someone to hunt, fish, and camp with as a boy. I had managed, with mother, through that. This was special. This was something rare between father and son. I felt his respect for me, too.

At twenty-two, I was at peace with my parents, with a mutual love and deep admiration.

Seeing that much, I suddenly saw something more. Here I was in the South Pacific, forging ahead with my life, making an adventure of it, hardly stopping to think about what brought me here. How can a child ever hope to repay the gifts from home?

* * *

I checked the time and discovered—Christ almighty!—it was four-thirty. My watch had ended a half hour ago. I "psss" at Steve, he stumbles up, smiling, groggy, saying, "Gidday, mate", and heads back to swing an arm around the backstay to relieve himself.

I can't go below yet. I sit up with Steve, back with the reality of the moment, of the ocean, of our journey. We talk about the States, about his traveling plans there, what he wants to see. After the sun makes a spectacular arrival, big and hot, I go to bed, curling up, cozy. All the memories had left me content, feeling solid, the present somehow tied together with the past to bring some meaning to the unknown direction I was going.

8. frustration island

**The Sailing Directions use the word
fantastic in reference to it.**

True, it lacks anchorages, because of steep reefs surrounding its twenty-five square miles—and that limitation may frustrate some sailors. But its 2,140-foot volcanic hills produce gorgeous, scenic "peaks and pinnacles." It has vegetation, lots of freshwater, a nice road around its circumference—real South Pacific amenities!

Rarotonga, largest of the eight Cook Islands, looked absolutely lovely to us when we sighted it on March 7. By the time we left, on March 13, we could hardly stand the place. The various things that had happened there during a

Motu (small isle) in the Bora Bora lagoon

four-day period included something to displease everyone. Not just me, not just the good guys, not even just the whole *Blue Orpheus* crew.

Frustrations began long before setting foot ashore. As we approached, the winds died. We could only stare longingly at the land so near and yet so far away. Jack briefly raised our hopes when he coaxed the engine into a spluttering start; then he reinforced his reputation as a jinx. Seeing what he thought was a leak, he shut the motor off again, and that was the end.

This had been our only shot at starting up, the battery was now dead, and there we were becalmed, ten miles from land.

On March 9, still becalmed, still within sight of Rarotonga, we asked ourselves, why? Why this undeserved punishment? We couldn't stand it. When the current began putting us toward the rocky lee side of the island, we hooked up the ship-to-shore radio and called the harbor. They sent a government boat out to tow us. We didn't care that it was a shoddy way to come in. We had had enough.

The news of our request spread very quickly. Before we reached Avatiu harbor, the local newspaper had a story in print, a follow-up of an earlier report on our troubles. I kept a clipping of that initial account, which read,

Yacht Battling Through
The yacht, the Blue Orchid

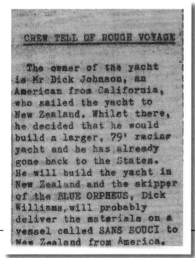

CREW TELL OF ROUGH VOYAGE

The owner of the yacht is Mr Dick Johnson, an American from California, who sailed the yacht to New Zealand. Whilst there, he decided that he would build a larger, 79' racing yacht and he has already gone back to the States. He will build the yacht in New Zealand and the skipper of the BLUE ORPHEUS, Dick Williams, will probably deliver the materials on a vessel called SANS SOUCI to New Zealand from America.

Local news

[sic], which got into difficulties on Thursday whilst en route to Rarotonga from Auckland was 500 miles south of the island when high winds blew out its mainsail. An electrical fire on board put the engine out of action and the crew of seven, two Americans, two Britons, and three New Zealanders, fought in heavy seas to fix the sail.

A further report was received on Friday when the vessel was 300 miles out and the mainsail had been repaired and replaced.

No other details are known except that the skipper's name is Dick. Both Barry Dundas, the ham radio operator who has been in contact with the yacht, and Don Silk, of Silk and Boyd, believe that the yacht will arrive either today or tomorrow.

When it was evident that the "Blue Orchid" had in fact battled through and was getting hauled into harbor, the *Cook Island News* spread the word at once:

Word was received late this morning that the Blue Orchid, the yacht traveling to Rarotonga from Auckland, was two and a half miles off shore and had asked for assistance. The Ravakai went to help the vessel into Avatiu as the yacht's engine was put out of action by an electrical fire some days ago. There are seven people on board the Blue Orchid, two Americans, two Britons and three New Zealanders. The yacht was expected to arrive at Avatiu Harbour at approximately 2 p.m.

Our reception began on a friendly note. Barry, our ham contact from Rarotonga, stood waiting at the dock. He repeated that a thousand-man Fiji search and rescue team, standing by, would have been activated the next day. We went to Barry's house to announce our safe arrival over the airwaves, and to have a joyous reunion from dry land with the networking "hams." (I'm eternally grateful for those guys and what they do.)

Thanks in good part to Carol and Rick, things began to go bad after that. The couple spent a very busy four days. I don't know whether they deliberately started out to make trouble, or just got wilder and angrier at us as they went along, because of their own disappointments.

Right off the bat, the day after our arrival, a reporter cornered Rick, Carol, and Lynn for a long news story. The account turned out to be reasonably fair and complete, with only minor errors like projecting a two-week stay in Rarotonga for the *Blue Orpheus* and saying a scuba tank had "blown up."

After loading the reporter's notebook, Rick and Carol proceeded to the "Banana Court" and Rarotonga officialdom, where they must have continued talking a blue streak for the next three days. Their goal was to get off the boat. They succeeded in doing a lot of unpleasant things, but not what they wanted most.

Immigration law specified that I, as Master of an Ocean Vessel, was responsible for getting them off the island, since I had delivered them. Visas would not be issued.

My responsibilities were politely explained to me, and I replied that the only way off Rarotonga I could provide was on the *Blue Orpheus*, which I was willing to do.

When Rick and Carol heard that I was "willing" to take them to Tahiti, they imitated our overheated scuba tank— blew up. They loudly protested against further travel in an "unsafe" boat, rehearsing stories of the storm, fire, and scuba tank.

Carol in particular was an active pain in the ass. After she had screamed at the immigration officials for a while, she would come and scream at me. Back and forth. But bureaucracy had spoken, and Carol lost. Her frustration was painfully great.

As for my own frustrations—most of the things I wanted to get done couldn't or wouldn't be done; things I didn't want to happen did happen; and I got a few new, nasty surprises. Rarotonga introduced me to a small world of bureaucratic complexities, and cut off my view of more interesting things.

Ordinarily, we might have expected a welcome into island life, but here we had only a glimpse or two. Evidence of dissension among the *Orpheus* crew probably caused the locals to keep their distance.

I don't mean that there weren't nice people around. The assistant harbor-master, William, a typically helpful, friendly Polynesian, introduced me to Ramaal, a beautiful French Tahitian girl. She showed me around the island, including a secluded swimming hole. Given the history of topless bathing in France, and the Bounty's experience with partly clad beauties, I should not have been surprised when she nonchalantly swam topless. Wow! The wonder of that moment stays with me to this day. I have never seen anything more perfect or tantalizingly gorgeous. We were touring on the boat's tiny motorbike, and after our swim I was more than happy to let her drive while I "held on" behind. She didn't seem to mind, and the remainder of the ride around the island was delightful!

A couple of times William's family also invited me to dinner at their home. A friendly American couple, Ray and Helen, invited me to their beach front home for dinner and company. And of course there was Barry, the ham operator. (But things went a little bad in that quarter. Carol had made a point of telling him I didn't have a license, and he cooled considerably after that. He made only a half-hearted attempt to fix the ham radio. I had been hoping we could leave Rarotonga with that instrument in good shape.)

Another frustration was the *Orpheus* repair. The island offered almost no facilities for fixing the boat—and we wouldn't have had money, anyway.

The government presented me with a one hundred dollar towing bill, which I was totally unprepared for. I didn't have a hundred dollars. DJ had promised money in Tahiti for supplies, but had sent us off with virtually nothing. I went round and round with the officials over the bill. Looking back, I can't believe I didn't have a hundred bucks. They didn't believe me, either, until we finally settled for everything I had—twenty-nine dollars.

I'm not sure what Jack was hoping for in Rarotonga, but he should have been the happiest—or least frustrated— person on the boat, seeing he got his way on a highly disputed point. But he climbed back on board rivaling Carol and Rick in sour looks.

He had absolutely insisted that the *Orpheus* had to carry two fire extinguishers. I thought that would be nice, if we had lots of money to spend. He couldn't care less if I was broke. That was my problem. We still had to take that precaution. In view of all my other problems and my empty wallet, I didn't exactly cheer his ultimatum, or respond very graciously. But what the hell. Maybe he had secretly bought into the "hex" idea, and was just planning to save our lives, in case the boat he was on got struck by lightning.

The only way I could comply was to go to the kiwis in desperation, and borrow forty dollars. So that pretty well completed the round of frustrations. The New Zealanders were generally a cheerful trio, so naturally we couldn't leave the island without finding a way to have them share our misery.

Goodbye, Rarotonga! Goodbye, goodbye, goodbye.

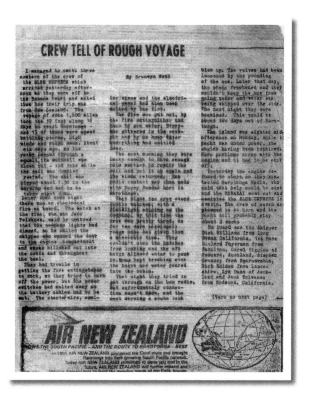

9. Tahiti—mutinies and bounties

"Oh, how does it feel,
to be on your own,
with no direction home,
like a complete unknown,
Like a rolling stone?"
—Bob Dylan

There are worse things than frustrations—for instance, threats on your life. Before we were out of sight of Rarotonga, Rick gave us that kind of undesirable surprise. He came out to the cockpit in a rage, finger pointing, hand shaking. He screamed, "Carol is not doing any cooking, I am not taking

Looking down on Papeete harbor and across to Moorea

any watches. We are staying in the forward cabin. If anyone comes up there or tries to force us to work, I have a gun and I will shoot you all, bang, bang, bang, bang, bang!"

I had seen eyes like that before, in the paranoid druggies walking into the Berkeley Free Clinic from off the streets. Experience had taught me not to argue. He was over the edge of sanity.

I remember feeling philosophically calm at the time, nodding my head, thinking, well, shit, nice to have you out of the way. If you stay put, in your cabin, that will shorten the six hundred-thirty nautical miles to Tahiti.

The seas and winds remained light throughout the eight-day trip, even after we hit the tradewinds two days out. We had comfortable sailing, making two adjustments to the absence of Rick and Carol. We ran two-man watches at night, both to illuminate the compass, and to protect the helmsman, just in case Rick lost what little was left of his self control.

Richard, as interim cook, showed prowess—at least, in creating rice "pudd." He would cook up an oversized pot to leave on top of the gimbaled stove. As watches changed we would inevitably linger over the stove to fill a bowl, or just dip a spoonful of the delicious stuff. I remember it with the same fondness I have for the good old Kiwi lingo itself: rice pudding is still "rice pudd" to me, and Richard's "ta," is still "thanks."

The boat continued to deteriorate. The steering hook-up from tiller to wheel broke for the third time, the instruments went out, so we were down to tiller, sails, and compass. Kind of nice, really, with a full moon, warm weather, and our rebellious passengers stashed away in the forward cabin.

* * *

Tahiti. On the evening of March 22 we sighted her dramatic blue hues—two indigo mountain patterns against about four shades of ocean water, with the sky splashing in another four or five colors—sunset gold, azure, twilight, and more.

The Society Islands are high, mountainous islands, covered with luxuriant vegetation to the summits and are well cultivated in the plains and valleys. There are numerous streams and cascades running down the sides of the islands into the sea.

Tahiti…33 miles long, northwest and southeast, and about 15 and a half miles wide…is formed by two ranges of high mountainous land…Mount Orohena, the highest mountain, is 7,339 feet in height… Papeete, the seat of the government of the Society Islands, stands on level ground with hills immediately behind it. With the exception of the wharf sheds and waterfront buildings, most of the town is screened from view by trees along the waterfront. The population was about 20,000 in 1968…

Minor [boat] repairs can be made. Diving gear and native divers are available…Fresh provisions can generally be obtained in limited quantity, but most vegetables are not recommended. Meat is scarce, except fish.

Sailing Directions for the Pacific Islands, 6th ed., III, H.O. Pub. 80, U.S. Naval Oceanographic Office.

Given fickle winds and confusing harbor lights, we hove-to all night (this consists of back-winding the jib and lashing the helm down to keep the boat more or less in one place).

The next afternoon we got a tow into the yacht harbor, this time from a private fisherman who gladly helped us.

Customs regulations require a boat entering another country to raise a yellow quarantine flag and remain on board until cleared. The natives of Tahiti didn't concern themselves much with formalities, though. They led us directly to the nearest bar.

From there I left the crew and went to the wharf to find "Dick," a "friend" of DJ's, my contact in Papeete. Obviously not that close a friend, Dick had little to say to me—just passed along a message from DJ to look up a guy named Bill at the hotel.

I couldn't believe what I saw. Bill was a sixty-year-old, hard-core alcoholic—a replacement for Jack! Evidently Jack and DJ had made a deal, DJ possibly guessing I would have needed Jack to get this far, but tension would be getting explosive by now. (If he did figure things this way, DJ wasn't far off.)

I never learned whether DJ had actually met this guy Bill, but, knowing DJ better by now, I think he could have taken on the three stooges, sight unseen. After all, the amazing crew he rounded up included Bill, Carol, and Rick as shipmates! (What would have happened if they had actually sailed together?)

My first night in Papeete ended very late, in the empty restaurant of a luxury tourist hotel. I had wandered in with only a few francs in my pocket, dirty, unshaven, not entirely sober. The waitress didn't just look beautiful to me—she acted beautiful. I asked what I could buy with my handful of French pennies.

She listened patiently to my story of the sail from

Auckland, and the problems along the way. Then she told me to order what I wanted. On the house; anything and everything. So I feasted. My last thought for the day was, "No wonder they call this place paradise."

* * *

The next day we cleared customs and got a tow over to the wharf and stern-tied with all the other yachts alongside main street Papeete. We would stay for twenty days, trying to recover from our near-disasters and make ready for the next leg. We began to empty and strip the *Orpheus* completely, to clean, repair, and reorganize.

But problems began immediately and continued throughout the first half of our stay. DJ had promised money would be waiting for us, but all we had got from him, at that point, was Bill. No money. Bill hung around the boat, embarrassingly drunk. I wondered how I would ever keep this guy from falling overboard.

Rick and Carol picked up where they had left off in Rarotonga. Along the wharf, they did their best to persuade everyone what dangerously unsafe, all-around bastards had landed from the *Blue Orpheus*. They also went down to immigration daily, trying to make me fly them out of the country. They would bring officials to the boat, then start screaming.

The officials would explain my obligation.

I would acknowledge. The couple had passage out the only way I could offer, on the boat. I didn't like it any better than anyone else. (After the officials got the picture, which didn't take long, the head man came and took me out for a beer, apologizing for the problems and sympathizing with me.)

Finally we reached DJ by phone. The conversation ended with a high-pitched discussion between him and Jack about the airline ticket DJ was supposed to send. I never understood the arrangement or the cause of the mix-up, but Jack got so mad at DJ for not sending him airfare that he lost control.

He took out his fury on me. Accusing me of being in cahoots with DJ, he first threatened me physically, but was just rational enough to know that line of conduct could get him into more trouble. He switched to the tactic of undermining my authority over the crew. He charged me with "inadequate leadership." During our engine fire at sea, he said, I had been on my knees praying, too scared to move.

Mutiny on the Bounty, Revisited, I thought. I never expected to play the part of Captain Bligh! Facing Jack, penniless, feeling wildly frustrated, I remembered the real scene, and how close we had come to losing the *Orpheus.* Instead of fighting the fire and physically doing everything I knew to save our asses, maybe I should have been on my knees, but any praying I actually did was wordless and after the fact.

Looking back years later, and trying to be fair, I suppose that in that confused scene Jack might actually have seen someone kneeling or getting down out of the smoke. But at the time, just after our communication with DJ, all I could see in Jack was dishonesty, utter disrespect, and distilled hatred. He had learned his new behavior pattern from Rick, or so it seemed. I didn't want either man on the boat another day—or another minute.

* * *

I didn't entirely get my wish, but that unpleasant exchange with Jack proved to be a turning point in our fortunes. Things began to improve. The first small blessing might have resulted from those turbulent scenes with Rick and Carol, and the latest confrontation with Jack. Bill decided to fly home—perhaps to get out of harm's way.

I hoped that Jack might follow suit, but, unable to get airfare from DJ to fly out of Tahiti, he stayed with us to Hawaii.

A week later Rick and Carol brought sunshine into our lives by leaving us, having made a deal with another boat for passage out. Naturally, we celebrated.

Next, DJ actually sent money that arrived just before I reached the level of desperation. The Kiwis were on the point of leaving. They had been hanging around a Norwegian freighter on the other side of the harbor, bumming meals, checking the routine, preparing to stow away. They really would have done that if DJ's dollars hadn't shown up.

A new starter came, too, and we could afford to replace the dangerously worn port aft lower shroud (shrouds, to a sailor, are not something to wrap a corpse in, just some support lines on the mast).

I hired an electrician to help me rewire the boat after the fire damage. He left before the job was done (paid in advance, of course), and I struggled to finish it alone without the know-how. Jack wasn't about to help.

Next, Lynn got on a boat headed for the Marquesas, leaving me with twinges of conscience. I don't think Lynn had any hard feelings, but I might have kept him on the

Orpheus if I had paid more attention to him, checking his morale and/or problems. He had just blended in—too well, maybe. I never took time to get to know him. So much else was going on, I never realized, until he took off, how I had ignored him.

Eventually, after about ten days of hard work from some of us, we had our boat back in good enough order to receive visitors. To my surprise, Rick's and Carol's slander seemed to have had the opposite effect from what they intended; with the *Orpheus* back in one piece, and more approachable, boaters began wandering by to get acquainted. We were making new friends.

Steve and Richard also provided a new attraction. They had met Belinda, a Kiwi doing a strip act at a local pub. When she began coming down to sunbathe on the boat in the afternoons, our popularity immediately increased multifold.

We saw less of Steve after he met a local beauty named Tina. When we did catch a glimpse of the two of them, we Americans could only grin and jealously shake our heads. Maybe we needed accents. Or access to some ancient Maori secrets.

* * *

We had the good fortune to meet a French doctor and his French-Tahitian wife who lived in a sumptuous place above Matavai Bay (where the Bounty once was anchored). Marlin Brando had stayed in the house during the film production, but the connection with actual history—Tahiti being where the Bounty actually anchored, and Christian actually lived—overshadowed the Hollywood interest.

The doctor had picked up Steve, Richard, and me as we were hitching back to Papeete from the Cascades Waterfall. Although the doctor's wife spoke little English, she provided gracious hospitality—dinner, entertainment, and eventually sleeping mats for an overnight stay. The couple pumped us for details of our voyage, and actually tried to get to know us.

Any time "older generation" people took us in and treated us as equals, I felt surprised. Us adults? Not really. Just faking it, and honored when "real adults" took us seriously.

You wouldn't mistake the house for King Tupou's palace, even though it sported a swimming pool. The setting made it special, though. Tropical fauna, exotic plants, ferns, and fruits surrounded the lawn. The view to the north showed all the colors of the sea, out far beyond Moorea. Directly east and below us lay the South Seas sailor's dream, Matavia Bay, with its colorful sub-surface reef, its beautiful beaches, its trees beyond. No wonder the Bounty crew opted not to leave paradise.

* * *

By this time we had acquired a more composite view of "paradise," though. Our introduction to island life in the Friendly Samoan Islands, on our way to New Zealand, had let us mingle with good people, full of love and life, innocence they never really lost, living for each day. No judging, no bandwagons…

But the Society Islands seemed more complex, a crazy quilt—like "society" itself. Even after our brief recent exposure I could count up a number of its segments.

Right off you would notice the French, and probably decide, as I did, that French-Tahitian must be the most beautiful mix of races, producing high cheekbones, creamy brown skin, delicate skeletal structure. Then it hurts you to know that where such beautiful people live, the French government decided to introduce the bomb. During our stay in Tahiti, tests were in progress, up to the northeast, in the heart of the warm living coral ocean.

You might wonder at the visibility of gay men, an equal and accepted group. The newspaper devotes a society page to them. You find their beauty contests publicly advertised. No closets in Tahiti.

You find two groups of boaters. Over on the north side the freighters and working boats have a purpose, a destination. Their people work for a living, without the time or the inclination to know and enjoy the rest of the populace or the land.

Among the sailors we mingled with I found (1) some trust babies, without a care or a purpose in the world; (2) some retirees from a fast corporate life who, having paid their dues and planned ahead, loaf along, appreciating flora and fauna, exploring the history of everything they see; (3) the young and poor—many owning their own boats, and not much else, and a few like us, crewing on something borrowed, leased, or on delivery, looking for adventure.

The tourists, the yachtees—not us—occupy the most visible and elegant facilities. They fly in, bus to the hotels, bake on the beaches, swim in the bay, eat in the tourist restaurants, walk the main streets, and fly back home.

Usually, I suppose, tourists don't have to get into the behind-the-scenes, "operating machinery" of the islands, but of course we did. To survive, we had to approach government offices as well as repair and supply facilities, and we had to perform a lot of drudgery ourselves.

Because of our casual friendships with the locals (allowing us, for instance, to spend the night in their homes when we had been out too late or were not sober enough to navigate back to the boat) we actually seemed to live out some tourist fantasies. Some locals we knew would generously share their secret swimming spots, or lead us to favorite cafes and bars. They must have had special toleration for, even sympathy with, impoverished people like us who couldn't fake or hide the state of our wallets.

* * *

At last we finished readying the *Orpheus*—a new starter installed, the alternator rebuilt, the wiring completed. We restocked with a lot of cans of baked beans, large cheap sardines, and rice and flour. Not exactly high class cuisine, but all we could afford with DJ's "generous" hand-out. At the last minute we would tie on to the boom and shrouds the usual bunches of green bananas and coconuts.

We still had an unsolved problem, though: no cook. We all understood what a tough job it could be, and we all knew we didn't want it. I had hoped the Kiwis might help us by persuading one of their several female friends to take on that duty in exchange for a ride to Hilo with us—but no. Instead, the Kiwis picked up Randy, promising he would provide occasional diversion. For starters, his name in New Zealand means "horny." Before long, he would be giving me the worst grief of the entire trip, but we started out from Tahiti on pleasant terms.

DJ had wanted us to bypass Hawaii (for reasons later apparent), and get to Los Angeles by way of the Marquesas. When the crew and I talked about it, we agreed that it looked like a hell of a long beat upwind from the Marquesas to California.

Jack and Steve put it more emphatically: it's Hawaii or we're not going. I had lost some faith in the boss by then, too, and we decided to hell with it, we're sailing through the Societies, up to Christmas Island, then up to Hilo. (I still regret not visiting the Marquesas, though—classic South Pacific fare, hundreds of atolls, all sizes, some inhabited, scattered throughout several hundred square miles.)

On our last night in Papeete, I guess the crew couldn't stand watching the tourists gorge on fancy food any longer. Some of them went and dined on a pricey dinner at one of the best restaurants in town, then split fast. I had to fish Randy and Richard out of jail the next day. The others somehow escaped the watchful eyes of the Gendarme, who had the boat pegged.

Obviously, we weren't always able to win the protection of "the locals," and there were times when we couldn't help feeling like beggars and social outcasts. Some people probably never have to endure such embarrassments throughout their whole lifetime. A good way to experience the predicament vicariously is to picture oneself as I once was, on the posh Italian Riviera—dead broke, without having eaten for two days. My fiancé and I couldn't bear to leave our tent and watch the tourists eat ice cream and enjoy the beach. We despised those gluttonous tourists (themselves, but not their money.)

As we untied the stern lines and motored out of the harbor, we were able to appreciate one shapely testimonial to the Kiwi's charm—a scantily clad female stood waving farewell to us. Tahiti was a hard place to leave even after three weeks. Maybe the land was beginning to hold more allure than the sea.

10. Moorea and Bora Bora

Moorea, only about ten miles from Tahiti, is less modernized, and features several mountains two to three thousand feet high.

Mount Tohivea reaches 3,975 feet. Another, Mount Mouaputa, has a hole completely through it near the summit, seen through on a southeasterly bearing. The island forms an equilateral triangle, each side about eight miles long. In 1956 the population was about 3,528.

Shortly after dark we calmly anchored in Robinson's Cove in Moorea, about two hundred yards from shore, with no anticipation of an immediate crisis.

Bora Bora at dawn

I jumped off the *Orpheus* and headed ashore, an easy distance for a reasonably strong swimmer. But Randy, not a reasonably strong swimmer, suffered, we soon would learn, from dangerously irresistible impulses. Seeing me dive in and head for shore, he suddenly turned into a humanoid lemming, it seemed, and, unbeknownst to me, blindly followed into the water.

The others on the *Orpheus* were inflating the rubber dinghy. After reaching land I turned to see Randy midway to shore, thrashing about in panic, and Steve desperately pumping up the half-limp raft.

Obviously Steve wasn't going to make it in time, so I jumped back in the water, and stayed under as I approached Randy. I spun his back to me, then surfaced to embrace him in a cross-chest carry. His nicotine-racked lungs produced a terrible, death-like stench.

When he recovered, Randy finally admitted that his stupid stunt almost cost him his life. But time would prove that unfortunately he hadn't learned to handle his potentially fatal impulses.

On this two-day stop I divided my time between enjoying solitude on the boat and enjoying company at the Bali Hai bar. Two interesting girls, Hina and Mareva, kept us occupied and entertained.

They told us about a wonderful sailing race that the bar sponsors each summer. At the start of each of the three days, the captain and crew must all down a huge Mai Tai, then run to the end of the dock or beach and swim to the boats anchored about fifty yards out. The race goes from Moorea to Raitea, Bora Bora, and Huahine, with each night ending with a feast and party on the beach, put on by the natives.

Trust the islanders to develop this kind of comforting competition. The losers probably end up feeling less pain than the winners.

DJ told me later that he knew the American who built the Bali Hai Hotels throughout Tahiti. The guy had outfitted a sailboat with the intent of sailing around the world, but decided Tahiti was good enough. He married a beautiful and rich Tahitian woman who was featured on tourist pamphlets and funded the hotels. The American eventually drank himself to an early grave.

* * *

We motored to Bora Bora, 140 miles, over ocean like glass, admitting to each other we didn't mind having the engine again. The Sailing Directions concede that this craggy place looks a little barren from the east. Coral reefs surround a group of islands that together enclose a central lagoon. Bora Bora Island, the largest, has two peaks rising slightly higher than two thousand feet. A dirt road around the island connects three small villages. Total population, in 1952, was about 2,000. What a quiet, laid-back, beautiful place. It offered hiking and picnicking, swimming and snorkeling, for an all too short two days.

The only disappointment came from our own crew— the ugly discovery that Randy's problems went beyond, much beyond, impulsiveness. I discovered some money missing, traced the problem to him, and confronted him. He confessed.

Two days later, while bound for Christmas Island, I learned that Randy was AWOL from the Coast Guard. Good Lord! As a final capper, the constantly seasick little s.o.b.

could not cook at all, much less take a watch at the helm. I wondered: Would the Coast Guard pay us to take him off their hands?

11. Christmas Island.
a gift from dolphins

After all the mountainous little places
we had been visiting, Christmas Island,
with a ninety-foot palm tree as its highest
landmark, imposed a worrisome contrast.

Twelve hundred miles from Bora Bora, near the equator, Christmas Island lies small and flat. Population, in 1964, was two hundred-fifty. Not a very big target.

Christmas Island stamps

DJ had suggested that I teach someone the basics of celestial navigation in the event something should happen to me. I had been trying to do that since leaving Auckland, with little success. Richard tried first, but had gotten too sick to concentrate on numbers. Steve gave up shortly after. Now Jack was willing to give it a go, working with me.

We had a few days of really nice sailing, six or seven knots with smooth seas, dolphins joining us almost every night. The fishing was terrible, though. We hadn't caught a thing since leaving Auckland. To make matters worse, the rice and flour from Tahiti had weevils. We sifted it, then cooked the hell out of it.

Our rotten mainsail ripped out again in some squally weather. The ham radio antenna gave constant headaches too. We would clip it to the fore and back stays, then haul it up on the spinnaker halyard. It broke regularly. Once it broke the halyard, which then proceeded to wrap itself around everything in sight.

That mess necessitated a trip up the mast in the boatswain's chair. The "chair" was basically a sling that was hooked to the main halyard so that some poor soul could be winched to whatever altitude was needed for repair or inspection of chafe points, spreaders, instrument sensors, broken rigging, etc. In a calm harbor it was merely a fear of heights that got one's attention. At sea, even a relatively calm one, it didn't take much altitude at all to feel the motion of the boat tenfold and cause one to cling to the mast with all one could muster! God how I hated that thing.

Making landfall at Christmas Island would be like passing a final qualifying test in navigation, by virtue of prevailing over cross currents, haze, and the low profile of the island.

On the day we should arrive, the haze had limited visibility to about two-and-a-half miles. Our awkward timing would make our noon sighting (to determine latitude) almost coincide with the estimated arrival time. I waited and waited for the noon sight, sitting on deck in the sun taking dozens of sextant shots, afraid of missing the zenith and somehow hoping I could make noon arrive earlier.

It finally came, in its own good time. I rushed below to reduce it. The fix put us at the exact latitude of the island, just a few miles east. We had to be sailing right by it in the haze! I directed the helm ninety degrees left, due west—a radical move, but I had no choice.

With binoculars, we spotted land within five minutes, but off the starboard beam, not directly ahead, a point of land in the haze. Our perceptions were off—I couldn't be sure how far away the point was—maybe two miles.

Then, suddenly, land appeared off the port side, about the same distance away. What the hell was going on? Where were we?

I was still buried in charts and sailing directions when someone hollered "Look at all the dolphins!"

Approaching from our four to five o'clock position swam a school of at least two hundred, more than we had ever seen before. Arcing never-ending rainbow profiles, they came right for us and surrounded our boat. We felt they had adopted us, made us a part of their school. And then, unmistakably, they turned us back to the north, east of the first point of land we had spotted.

We never questioned what they were doing. We were quite mesmerized by what was happening, and confused about our exact position anyway.

But it became clear as we approached the point of land. A low beach appeared in the haze, connecting both tips of land. We had been sailing directly into the Bay of Wrecks—a place well named after seeing how many old ship hulks lay rotting on the bottom. The conditions we had were typical. The haze and low U-shaped bay have suckered a great many vessels into that lee shallows to run aground. Like the *Orpheus*, they might have been steered by men in the act of congratulating themselves on their navigational skills. Why did the beautiful dolphins choose to protect a scraggly crew like ours?

The dolphins led us completely around the north shore of the island, and then as we made our final course change to the south for the lagoon on the west side, they left us, squeaking a deafening farewell.

We sat in stunned silence, except for Richard. He was muttering softly. There were a few familiar whispered expletives, I thought, then some long pauses. Finally the master just sat there, silently shaking his head.

I don't think even the most cynical of us can ever forget or fail to cherish that "spot of time." It wasn't just the encounter with life forms as intelligent as human beings— and in their own element, more powerful. We had seen for ourselves the compassionate, caring behavior of those forms. That evidence persuades me that something greater than man or anything else on earth exists elsewhere—has put all this together, made sense of it, and added a mysterious element of beauty.

We already loved the dolphins and felt a kinship to them, but this was a new lesson. They had interacted with us at our human level. Perhaps they had lowered themselves in the process, but we appreciated it.

* * *

The Captain Cook Club offered warm Australian beer and electric lights a couple of hours a day. The village consists of that and one store with half-filled shelves, the police station, and the post office with a radio station.

The population here used to be over ten thousand during the atomic tests from 1954 to 1958. A United States World War II base had left behind a number of barracks and old signs, as well as five runways. The natives came from the Gilbert and Ellis Islands, and the whites were British.

Like the natives on all the little out-of-the-way islands we saw, the Polynesians were very friendly. They asked us to feasts everyday and planned outings to take us out to the reefs fishing and diving. One particularly memorable dinner was an unknown species of sea bird that rivaled a super ball for bounce. The two Britons seemed to enjoy their authority but the natives simply ignored them. For the most part, so did we.

The P.O. asked us to deliver the mail to Hilo for them, On Her Majesty's Service. The second of two ships a year was not due for a long time. As part of the deal, the native postmaster gave us complimentary postcards, stamps, and postmarks, and our own mail with the Christmas Island postmark went into the sealed mail pouch.

12. time to reconsider

My months in the South Pacific were evidently beginning to take their toll.

Maybe the problems we had encountered getting this far were catching up with me. Maybe I was picking up secret warnings about the worst crisis of all, waiting for us on the next leg. Or perhaps I was subconsciously thinking of the long arm of the United States Coast Guard, reaching out after a fugitive we—innocently—happened to have aboard. (And I suspected there might be other problems with the Coast Guard—DJ had rather carefully avoided them, it seemed to me.)

Whatever the cause, I had reached a low point—was feeling depressed and jaded, at the very moments when I had received a nice gift of time—a little freedom to relax and/or meditate during an interval of ideal weather, with perfect sailing conditions ahead.

I began to focus on the drawbacks and failures of island life. The beautiful people we encountered, though friendly and happy, had slight education, few books, almost no stimulation—little to do but gather coconuts and fish.

But the world I grew up in, one of over-stimulation, creates major stresses and frustrations. I remember reading about the wide variances between what people say is important to them and what they actually do. They typically complain about not having time for what they really want. Are they perceiving their wants inaccurately, or are they having minor time-management problems, or are they overwhelmed by society's demands and norms? Maybe today's urban world has become incompatible with the human soul, blocking it from where it wants to be and what it wants to do.

One great advantage of South Pacific islanders may lie in their freedom from time stress problems. For these islanders, so much more relaxed than the people who visit them, time stress neuroses and all such psychological problems remain almost totally unknown. The natives seem to be in closer touch with their souls—or at least with their sources of happiness. But must the price be ignorance and isolation?

It occurred to me that, in the process of sailing through the South Pacific I had become aware of three perspectives on time. First was the outlook I had grown up with, observing working stiffs for whom time is a series of eight-hour days, forty hours a week, with haphazard priorities filling in the remaining spaces. In contrast with that, the islanders do everything they can to ignore time and its perimeters.

But the demands of navigation had taught me a third way of perceiving and working with time. I had become intrigued by its astronomical uses—measurements of coordinated movements of planets, suns, and moons, from which human clocks and calendars are derived. How habitually people isolate themselves from that background! Society has managed to reduce a vast cosmic dance to the level of chronologies and daily schedules.

I resolved not to forget that cosmic dance.

* * *

Three months had gone by since we left Auckland—such a brief period. In that interval I had faced more problems and headaches than in my entire previous life. (Probably made more mistakes too, dealing with people. An analysis of my leadership qualities did not make me feel particularly good, but it seemed that our problems had not really been **anyone's** fault.)

My primary concern had been to operate the boat safely, which with my inexperience had taken virtually all my time at sea. The crew came second. Where a professional could perhaps have handled both responsibilities expertly and deftly, I often used no finesse in bluntly getting to a point. I paid for my tactlessness. Out of the seven persons who had been with me since Auckland, only two liked me. Two might have felt indifferent, but three probably hated my guts.

As a landlubber I never anticipated one paradox in a sailor's life. At the very moment you are seemingly the freest, out amidst the bounding, boundless waves, you are actually confined within a closed society, tighter than anything you find on land. That restriction must surprise and confound some new sailors.

It's not just a closed society, either; according to ancient tradition, it's also a dictatorship, benevolent or otherwise. In modern times a green captain might find that structure difficult to handle, perhaps undesirable. But he abandons it at everyone's peril. Certain things on a boat simply won't work by majority rule. When conditions—sometimes, emergency conditions—call for quick sail changes or instant helm movements, nothing could be less appropriate than a democratic discussion of their advisability.

Squabbles about handling the *Orpheus* never occurred, though. My sailing orders were pretty solid and never questioned. The crew trusted my navigation.

I wasn't a tyrant, and didn't try to run a dictatorship. We would discuss routings and change them if common sense, economy, and personal preferences, all weighed together, so indicated. No one objected to the relatively easy duty schedules I worked out. Everyone understood that we had only a fixed amount of dollars—very few—to work with.

Eliminating problems of boat management and dictatorship brought me back again to our confined situation, and related fears. If a crew member has decided he didn't want to be aboard, and can't do anything about getting away, he can at least take consolation in hating somebody for his captivity. What better person to hate than the boss?

We had all lived through the "hippie" movement of the sixties. "Non-" and "anti-" society people react unpredictably when forced into a tight organization like that of a small boat. Some may want a totally tight dictatorship. Others may rebel at having to be a part of a society at all, and try to remain un-established.

But neither of those options really works. For a small boat like the *Orpheus*, you need a benevolent leader who has had a chance to take a key action before the crew begins to be tossed around together at sea: assemble a crew whose members know each other well and will be compatible in unusual circumstances. And everyone must understand what remains open to majority rule or discussion, and what does not.

If the skipper can't assemble a crew that already knows one another, the skipper's survival could depend on his ability to evaluate strangers. "People-reading" skill probably matters more to a skipper than anything else, except navigation.

Those thoughts didn't exactly console me, considering I was now stuck with a crew that, except for a couple of sturdy fellows, had been just handed to me. I didn't much regret the way I had dealt with problems, once they had come up; but I did wish I had been able to anticipate and avoid some of the conflicts to begin with.

The crazy thing for me was, it all seemed worthwhile. I suddenly realized that I had gained a great deal. I had grown. I had learned a lot, in spite of a loneliness I wouldn't have believed possible.

Sitting on the beach, still alone, watching the *Orpheus* with the sun going down behind it, an outrigger coming in over the reef, our dinghy on its way out with some crew—I felt like a character in a storybook fantasy. Christmas Island had presented me a large, precious, spot of time.

The next day the only other yacht around, a trimaran with two families on board, headed out for Hilo. We never saw them or heard of them again, even after our own eight-day stay in Hilo. We left Christmas just a few hours after them. We had another fright with Jack first. He stepped on a sea urchin while swimming out to the boat at night, and his yells plus a commotion in the water near the boat convinced us that sharks had done him in. It turned out to be manta rays slapping the water.

13. man everboard!

The engine went kaput for the final time.

We got a contaminated fuel line again, and during the long, painful bleeding process I found a permanent "solution" to the problem: I accidentally broke the head off a bleeding nipple. We had no replacements or plugs. After this final curse we sailed, in the pure sense of the word, from then on.

Heading north from Christmas Island we enjoyed the pure sailing as we relaxed in excellent weather, with only occasional squalls, and operated pretty well together as a crew. Given the time and conditions to get to know each other, finally, we spent hours in the cockpit talking about our lives, countries, and plans after the voyage. The Kiwis and I thought we might do some traveling together around the United States.

By then Jack had mellowed out enough, even, to express a wish to try his hand at navigation. I encouraged him, and let him handle most of the work on the Hawaii-bound leg.

Randy, we generally forgot about. Since his failure as a cook Richard had pretty well taken over the galley, doing his best with our marginal Tahitian provisions. And Randy's prowess as a sailor was about on a level with my mastery of ballet dancing.

The crew and I had been playing around a little bit, honing our skills, sailing up to and gaffing Japanese fishing balls. After several days' practice without an engine we had acquired a collection of sizes from four-inch diameters up to about fourteen-inch balls. We were picking up quality merchandise, the old blown glass type, covered with shells and barnacles. Most of them still had netting attached.

Toward evening, one ball happened to give us a particularly bad time. In a strong open water current, 400 miles from land, working against three-foot choppy seas, I missed four or five passes in a row. We just couldn't find an approach angle that would get us closer than thirty feet or so. Fed up, I called off the operation.

Someone said, "Well, whoever wants that one will have to go in after it."

As I headed down to the cabin I heard someone gasp incredulously, "No!"

I turned just in time to see Randy dive headlong into the sea and dog paddle toward the ball.

It took us a couple of seconds to react. My first thought was, "If we couldn't sail up to the damned ball, what made Randy think we could sail up to retrieve him?"

"Drop the sails! I'm going after him," I yelled, tying the nearest line around my waist and jumping in. "Give me more line!"

Two crew jumped up to the halyards while Richard worked on more line. But after quickly reaching the end of my tether I could only catch brief receding glimpses of Randy's arm above the waves, as the powerful current separated us.

"Haul me in!" I had to yell to be heard above the commotion. "We'll have to raise sail to get back up to him."

As I was scrambling back aboard, Jack and Richard leaped for the main halyard—but couldn't quickly sort out the tangled mess of lines.

"Forget it. Hoist the jib."

By then Steve and I, desperately looking around for Randy, suddenly realized with a terrible gut-wrenching jolt that we had lost him—out in a 360° horizon with nothing to get a bearing on.

After what must have been several minutes and seemed several hours, looking every direction, ground down by the horrible sinking possibility that we had lost Randy forever, Steve finally spied a waving arm about three hundred yards off the starboard beam.

Amidst noises that seemed deafening I screamed to Steve that he must stay on the bow and not take his eyes off Randy.

With our jib trimmed up, heading over to him, we soon realized we couldn't get close enough against the current, given the wind direction and our current tack.

My heart was probably beating three or four times its normal rate. I never wished more desperately for a working motor. And I was in too much of a hurry, afraid of losing sight of Randy again.

I got the wrong angle downwind from Randy after sailing past him. His eyes had burned themselves on my brain as we had come within thirty feet. They had the look of a man who knew he might die very soon, and knew his life depended completely on the mercy and skill of another.

When we came about I soon saw that the new tack wouldn't work any better. The sun, dropping low on the horizon, blinded us from the west. I cursed the engine for failing us altogether just before we needed it most.

If darkness came before we succeeded in getting Randy, he would die, alone, at sea, soon after giving up and letting go of his fishing ball prize.

We made a seemingly endless number of tacks. I couldn't figure out a solution. We were sailing circles around Randy, coming close on every tack, but not close enough. My fear of losing him affected my ability to think clearly, and to judge exactly what the conditions were doing to us. I tried a couple of Richard's and Steve's suggestions, which didn't work either.

Richard and Jack finally got the main up. In retrospect, I think the current was so forceful that the jib just couldn't make headway against it, and I did not take time, at first, to size up the geometry of the wind and current.

But with the main in place, we had new hope. I adjusted our tack once more and had Jack, our strongest crew swimmer, get ready to jump overboard wearing a life jacket and carrying an extra. He would have a line around his waist, with plenty of extra length.

I told the crew, "We keep a little speed up as we sail next to Randy. Jack jumps in and grabs him. I turn upwind, Richard and Steve drop sails. We'll be ready to haul in Randy and Jack."

We got in position to come up on Randy on a starboard close reach. Jack stood poised. In spite of the growing darkness, we had a fighting chance.

Steve gave me a perfect turn in for the tack, watching Randy, looking backwards from the bow pulpit. When Steve was sure I had Randy in sight and wouldn't lose him, he readied himself at the mast halyards. Richard was standing by to let go of the jib and mainsheets. The thought flashed across my mind that soon two men would be in the water. We would pass within ten feet of Randy, but going fast.

"Now!" I bellowed, but Jack was already on his way. Richard released the sheets just as I turned into irons, and

Steve madly tore the sails down. Jack had Randy in a vise-lock grip. They were off the ball.

Then Richard was hauling them in. I gave a hand. We landed Randy first, then Jack. Once they were in, the cockpit became strangely quiet as we all sat panting, catching our breath.

* * *

At last Randy spoke. "Well, I guess you guys will each want a turn," he said as he bent over and presented his backside for boots to the ass. Nobody replied or moved in response to the feeble attempt at humorous apology. No one even wanted to talk to Randy, much less allow him to direct the action—any more than he already had. After a few embarrassed seconds of silence, Randy returned upright and then took a seat in the cockpit.

Finally a few words emerged, mostly exclamations and curses.

"Jesus Christ."

"Son of a Bitch!"

"That wasn't very fucking smart, Randy."

When he was finally spoken to, Randy began to babble. "I know, I know, I can't believe I did it. I'm sure glad you guys got me back in. For a minute I thought you'd lost me."

"We had."

Silence followed as that announcement soaked in and the little swimmer revisited the vision he had had of death's bright angel.

"God damn it, Randy, that better be the last time." He glanced at us then lowered his gaze. Even he might have realized that saving a man's life once a week could get tiresome for the rest of us—though, as I sat marveling at the guy, I wondered whether he was suicidal or just too idiotic to understand what he was doing to us.

We couldn't move for awhile. Then we mechanically and silently began cleaning up lines and hoisting the sails. By the time we were under way again, darkness had settled in. We spent a very quiet evening.

The intense moments just before sunset must have been replayed in all our minds as we tried to understand and accept them. How would we feel if we were sailing on now without Randy? Or how would it feel to be alone in the ocean, watching the *Orpheus*'s mast and sails disappear under the horizon forever?

My brain felt burned out. I couldn't keep a thought in my head for more than a few seconds before flitting on to something unrelated. I didn't have the energy to even move and focus my eyes.

14. celebrity interviews and a grand entrance

From that point on, a tired, bored crew found the cruise to Hilo "forgettable."

Jack had under-compensated for drift, so the land we sighted on May 16 was the southwest tip of the big island. Getting to Hilo from that point meant hard sailing along the coast.

The sailing directions had warned that the trades split up at the northeast tip of the island and scream southward down the shore. Lacking auxiliary power, we couldn't go the lee side and risk getting becalmed. So we went beating up the coast for seventy-two miserable hours, fighting twenty-five to thirty knot winds, thirty-degree heels, and hammering seas. We made innumerable tacks.

I found myself watching the boat closely, suspecting interior weakening. We could actually watch the deteriorating effects of salt, water, and wind on the surfaces of the *Orpheus*, and it stood to reason that the basic structure would be eroding, too.

Three days of going against nature east of Hawaii seemed hardly more comfortable than three days of enduring a tropical storm had been. But our approach to Hilo offered less of a mental strain. We had freedom of choice, after all; we could abandon the tack at any time, and the end was in sight.

* * *

Richard came up into the cockpit one evening, feeling good, phony microphone in hand, spouting forth a very proper British accent: "Richard Fayerman, BBC, here, on board the infamous yacht *Blue Orpheus* with her courageous crew, applauded worldwide for their incredible voyage from Down Under, New Zealand. I have here Steve Gregory, Maori guide and island playboy. What do you think of the trip so far, Mr. Gregory?"

"Bloody nightmare."

"Um, er, righto. Any specifics on that?"

"The boat is a pile of junk. The food stinks. The cooking is bloody awful." Steve and Richard (the volunteer part-time cook) stared at each other briefly, neither one changing expression. "The women in Tahiti were wonderful, though."

"Yes. Well, perhaps we'd better move on to other crewmen. Randy, has your background in seamanship given you a different view? Perhaps you'd like to take this moment to greet your old friends in the United States Coast Guard?"

Randy looked extremely uncomfortable, and finally blurted out, "Thanks. I'm just glad to be here."

"Ah, yes. I understand perfectly. And now, how about Mr. Jack?"

"The real fun for me was the fire. I really wanted to get the chance to inflate the life raft. I was dying to see it if would really inflate, and what DJ's design entailed for survival equipment. I bet it would have been terribly entertaining."

"Right, yes. Perhaps you will still get your wish. And now, what about you, Captain?"

"What can I say? With a motley crew like this, and the kind of equipment you see, I am amazed to be here.

"I'd like your audience to understand, though, that I'm really proud of these motley seamen. The world knows them as the crew that's hard as nails. The only mystery to me is why these nails are always screwing up."

"Thank you, Captain. And there you have it, folks, the infamous, dirty buggers who call themselves sailors on the *Blue Orpheus*, who have braved wild women and native seas—oops, other way round—unfriendly pissers, and other terrible unforeseen circumstances, are triumphantly about to arrive in the great old U.S.A.!

"Richard Fayerman, BBC, aboard the *Blue Orpheus*, returning you to London as the crew here stands by, humming 'Rule, Britannia!'"

* * *

After we finally rounded the point on May 18, the wind went from surfeit to starvation. We lay becalmed in sight of land. Squall after squall moved through, giving us spurts of momentum. Finally in early afternoon a squall put some good air on our stern and we went for it, right into harbor. It was a very impressive piece of sailing. We timed the ninety degree turn into the harbor just right, maneuvered around several other boats, made some quick sail changes, and, to cap our precise coordination, made a spectacular mooring.

After all the bad things we had been through, it did us a world of good to do everything right in front of a big audience. The harbor was right in front of town.

15.Hilo: winners, losers

We spent ten days in Hilo, an unusual, genuine-seeming place, off the tourist route. Even in our short stay we saw an odd mixture of factions and attitudes—not exactly the view the Waikiki visitor gets.

The Hawaiians didn't seem to like whites. Disillusioned with Waikiki, they venerated their relatives in the private places of Hawaii, where pure Hawaiian blood still exists, unmixed with European or Asian strains. In addition, Orientals seemed unfriendly toward Hawaiians—and sometimes Caucasians as well.

Stern tied in the Hilo harbor

A new group of unlovely whites happened to be visible in force then, the so-called Jesus freaks, a confrontational group who stopped busy pedestrians in their tracks, to learn whether those brothers and sisters were on the path to salvation. I thought their conversion techniques grew out of the kind of love and compassion the old Spanish Inquisitors used to spread. Richard decided, and I tended to agree, they were "a bloody (six expletives deleted)...pain in the arse." They probably did more damage to the reputation of whites than "typical tourists" did.

We felt the three-way racial tensions every time we went into a bar or small store, and that undercurrent made us uneasy. But somehow we continued to form friendly relations with the locals.

Late on the 18th, our first day in Hilo, I swam ashore and went to customs, which was closed. So was the post office. But I did find a shower and shave, ice cream, candy, and a newspaper.

A lot of people had watched our flawless entry, our silent handling of sails, and talked about the show we put on. Many of them no doubt thought not using our diesel had been a matter of choice! When some new acquaintances learned otherwise, they proved helpful. Impressed with the sailing skills of the *Orpheus* crew, and sympathetic with our problems, they towed us through the narrow channel to the wharf where we stern tied next to the Coast Guard. They also supplied us with food and beer until we cleared customs and could officially leave the boat.

Crew changes began at once, beginning with Randy's departure. I never would have believed that we would actually be looking him up later, but that's what happened.

He had wanted us to come in after dark and drop him off in the water where he could swim to shore (Ha!) but we didn't oblige him. After we had tied up, though, and I was in the head, he sneaked off the boat without a witness before customs came. We rejoiced—prematurely.

Soon we discovered that our good buddy had taken some more of my money, a pair of boots, and a shirt. We easily tracked him down, with the help of some lowlifes he had stolen money from too. Being away from the boat, and thoroughly fed up with the thief by then, I let myself get a little physical as well as verbal. After slamming him against a wall, I said a number of unpleasant things to the guy I had saved once from drowning, and the whole *Orpheus* crew had worked frantically to rescue again.

He broke down, admitted guilt. And I felt sure he'd steal from us again, given the chance. I'm sorry I hadn't read, at that time, a remark of Mark Twain's. I would have repeated it to Randy, as a parting thought: *"If you pick up a starving dog and make him prosperous, he will not bite you, which is one difference between a dog and a man."*

Jack didn't leave until plane fare arrived from DJ, two days before we left Hilo. In the meanwhile we found three new crew members. Finally, for the last leg of the journey, I would have my own choice of shipmates.

An American couple, Dan and Nancy, could fill in for Richard on the galley. I didn't expect much boat handling help from Dan, a tall, skinny, vegetarian hippie. But his girl looked competent, more realistic about life and sailing.

Another American, the third addition, turned out to be a jewel: another Steve—Steve M., an easy-going, friendly, experienced sailor from San Bernardino.

* * *

Well I got back
and took the parking ticket off the mast
I was ripping it to shreds
when this Coast Guard boat went past.
They asked me my name,
and I said Captain Kidd.
The funniest thing was
as I was leaving the bay
I saw three ships a sailing
they were all headed my way.
I asked the captain what his name was
and how come he didn't drive a truck
he said he was Columbus
and I just said good luck.

—Bob Dylan's 115th Dream

We thought we had permanently parted company with our old "friends" Rick and Carol, but we thought wrong. Five days after our arrival in Hilo, they showed up in Hilo, aboard the *Westerly*. Rick smugly wagged his finger at me, with an evil smile. It was going to be Rarotonga and Tahiti all over again, except this time the repercussions would continue a lot longer. The couple's first stop, of course, would be the Coast Guard office to file a complaint against us.

Later that afternoon, a Coast Guard officer came to visit the boat. Surprise, surprise. Polite and professional, he conducted a routine safety inspection. He faulted me mildly for placing the boat's registration placard at the wrong location.

He went on into Rick and Carol's specific complaints, including one that we had blown a hole in the hull when a scuba tank exploded. We both chuckled at the absurdity of that, and the officer soon realized my problems had originated with Rick and Carol. The inspection ended with me getting an official nod of approval from the United States Coast Guard.

He left me with a very uneasy feeling, all the same. Though I escaped censure, I wasn't so sure about DJ's status. The officer had quietly noted that DJ might have some violations, which weren't my problem. He didn't elaborate—just told me to stay in port.

By luck, I reached the ever-elusive DJ by telephone in Los Angeles. He promised to send, right away, the money I needed for food and supplies. He graciously accepted our need to sail to Hawaii, in spite of his advice to the contrary. He even pointed out another advantage in our being in Hilo. His *Nam Sang* would soon arrive. I could meet the crew, exchange some equipment with them, and "give them a little help with their navigation."

But when I told him about the Coast Guard inspection, he came unglued. "Good God! Dick," he exclaimed, "get the hell out of there!" He mentioned some previous hassles with the Guard, said we were dealing with a bunch of idiots. I just couldn't waste any time in getting out of that port. I had never before heard him that excited, or that emphatic.

Eventually I would understand why he might have had very good reasons to fret. DJ was continuing to be a mysterious but romantic character. What kind of "business dealings" had led to this exhibition of near-panic? Not only that—how far was he asking me to stick out my own neck?

Idiots or not, the USCG could put on a pretty majestic show sometimes.

But anyway, I promised that as soon as we had money for supplies we would stock up and leave. I guess DJ knew he could count on our common distaste for bureaucrats.

* * *

May 25: The *Nam Sang* arrived three days before we left Hilo. It was a big boat, with a crew obviously green as hell. (DJ had warned me what to expect, and asked me to help them with charts and navigation.) It scared me to realize how much they didn't know. They didn't know how to use their sextant, a plastic student model. They didn't understand navigation—they had followed jet contrails to find Hawaii. DJ had chartered the *Nam* to them bareboat—fourteen poor souls. We gave them the mini-bike, charts, a spinnaker pole, assorted odds and ends, and wished them luck. Later we read about them:

> *The dismasted 73-foot American sloop Nam Sang arrived in Auckland today, after limping 500 miles under auxiliary power to port... On July 2 in 32-foot waves and 40 knot winds a stay broke causing the 70-foot aluminum mast to collapse... The mast snapped, damaging railings and the gunwale. The crew used bolt cutters to jettison the mast and the sloop motored to New Zealand with its small auxiliary motor. The Nam Sang took four months to travel from Long Beach. It was the second time the 40-year old Nam Sang was dismasted in heavy seas off the New Zealand coast. The previous dismasting happened in 1965.*

Bad luck? At least they evidently did better than the trimaran that left Christmas Island just ahead of the *Orpheus*. Bound for Hilo, it never arrived. After receiving a "missing" report, the Coast Guard had checked other possible ports with no further clues. Those trimarans have a terrible reputation for falling apart at sea, just as the *Nam* seems to have a habit of losing its masts. Its latest survivors might be thinking of themselves as the "lucky fourteen."

* * *

May 26: Money came from DJ. We restocked for the long sail to the mainland. I worked on the engine until three-thirty a.m. but found it unfixable, lacking the right parts. I gave it up.

So Lady Luck had given us a terrible time with our motor power. Would she compensate or take pity, and reward us in other ways? The sages warn us not to count on her capricious friendship. Spurn her, and she seems to beg for trust. Depend on her, and the Lady may suddenly scorn you, even maliciously put venomous snakes in your path.

But the boundless sea, and the boundless air, produce superstitious people. Those two uncontrollable elements, as massive and strong as the earth itself, make sailors and fliers feel insignificant while bobbing along in them. As we bob along, the scientists and logicians who deny her existence look no more dependable than Lady Luck herself, and just as insignificant as we.

Shortly before we left Hilo, friends gave us a Ti leaf, to ward off evil. The natives say one should never be destroyed or transplanted or bad luck will follow. We strapped it so tightly to the backstay that a pitchpole would not have dislodged it.

* * *

May 28: We left Hilo at two p.m. We had to get a tow through the breakwater channel out to the harbor, an absolute humiliation in contrast to our sail in.

The captain of the fishing boat I hired didn't know what he was doing. He dropped the tow line in a critical spot and had us heading for shallow water. We scrambled to drop anchor and tried again. What did he do but repeat the same stunt, leaving me livid with frustration!

Of course the usual entourage, the Kiwi Fan Club, was standing by to wish us bon voyage, and watching our fumbles. We finally got out into the harbor and happily began sailing under wind power.

The Hilo crew, with Ti leaf on backstay

16. the long last lap

It never occurred to me to worry about Coast Guard problems facing me on the mainland, if I got that far.

But I did worry some about the chances of a safe arrival. I hoped for a little compassion from Lady Luck—or at least non-interference.

On the minus side, we had 2,400 miles to negotiate in a sailboat that sure wasn't what she used to be, and even lacked a usable motor. If we ran into the kind of trouble the *Nam* had, and got dismasted 500 miles from port, the news stories about us would have a different and grimmer ending.

Watching Richard do some sail mending (double exposure)

We had three new, untested crew members, Nancy, Dan, and Steve M. We had mediocre food supplies for just twenty-four days, and we could get very hungry.

On the plus side, we had two veteran crew members who had proved themselves in emergencies, and a new man who looked like an improvement over his predecessor. If Jack had been jinxed, we had left him behind, and had acquired a lucky Ti leaf. As a skipper I had learned to cope with several kinds of crises. We could expect some favorable winds on our planned route. We had an extra supply of water.

It didn't take long to discover that Nancy could have been a great asset. She had real cooking talents, without much food to work with. Her man Dan fit the pattern of other cooks' partners—a poor to lousy sailor. You could well believe that Carol and Rick had left me gun-shy. I bypassed the cook and her consort as much as possible—even avoided them.

Among our assets, I shouldn't overlook Richard's gifts in the art of profane self expression, a useful morale factor. He spoke for us, and relieved our frustrations by means of his x-rated comments on squalls, bad food, too much wind, too little wind, bad visibility, scorching sunshine, and all such discomforts. Long before our last leg, during some heavy weather, a wave found its way directly through an open hatch onto my head; my serious apprenticeship under Richard began at that moment.

Our trip started off with such mild, favorable weather that Richard had very little to swear at. Our new man, Steve M., got right into a study of navigation, and I gladly taught him, thinking that here was another sailing mate whose friendship I'd like to maintain in years to come.

No engine meant no charging of the batteries. We saved them for the electric bilge pumps and radio. We rigged a kerosene lamp for light in the cabin at night. The glass was a spice jar cut open, the shield was a tin can lid.

Although we had caught plenty of fish on the way to New Zealand, we hadn't caught anything but bubble balls since leaving Auckland. So it was time to get serious. When none of our commercial lures succeeded we developed our own. Richard took a plain three-pronged hook, shredded one of my old college tie-dyed sheets, attached it, wrapped a little tin foil on top, and started catching fish almost immediately.

Richard's lure attracted more than fish. An albatross spotted it and hovered over it constantly. We named him Alby and grew fond of him. After a few days he either went to get a fish near the lure or got caught by it. We found him drowned one morning at the end of the line, our initial excitement at believing we had caught a fish turning to horror as we pulled him in. He had become a friend who had stayed with us through good and bad weather.

A frightening silence prevailed as we grieved for Alby and also ourselves, remembering the *Ancient Mariner:*
> *...At length did cross an Albatross,*
> *Through the fog it came;*
> *As if it had been a Christian soul,*
> *We hailed it in God's name.*

> *It ate the food it ne'er had eat,*
> *And round and round it flew.*
> *The ice did split with a thunder-fit;*
> *The helmsman steered us through!*

> *And a good south wind sprung up behind;*
> *The Albatross did follow,*

And every day, for food or play,
Came to the mariners' hollo!

In mist or cloud, on mast or shroud,
It perched for vespers nine;
Whiles all the night, through fog-smoke white,
Glimmered the white Moon-shine. "

"God save thee, ancient Mariner!
From the fiends, that plague thee thus!—
Why look'st thou so?"—With my crossbow
I shot the Albatross...

And that, as S. T. Coleridge told the tale, started BIG TROUBLES. Since we had no malicious intentions, the powers must have decided to spare our lives, but we did get becalmed.

With our lives literally depending on the wind, I developed love-hate feelings bordering on the maniacal. First I despised a dangerously destructive wind raging out of control, screaming, boiling the water into huge waves. Now after it left us, leaving our sails listlessly, uselessly snapping, we all ached for a touch of the wind I hated, with helpless fear approaching panic. The ocean surface became a strange moving mirror. How could we help but think about running out of food and water, and even about trying to paddle to shore? The only respite was to swim 1,200 miles from anywhere in 19,000' of water above the "moonless mountains".

But when the wind would freshen and fill the sails, and the boat would take on the sounds and feels of movement, we couldn't help thanking something or someone, or the wind itself. For a chance to live.

But our thanks would have a bitter taste. Being so completely dependent leaves you both worshipful and resentful toward such a fickle bitch.

Old sailors say that only one in nine days is ideal for sailing. I believe that's a fair mathematical summary. One day in nine you're comfortably in love with the wind and the sea; the other days you're trying to figure them out, and sometimes fighting them for your life. I guess people relationships are similar. "Can't live with women, can't live without them." (I suppose women say that about men, too). The love and hate that make the world go round.

> *I was sittin in the bathtub,*
> *counting my toes,*
> *when the radiator broke*
> *water all froze*
> *I got stuck in the ice*
> *without my clothes*
> *naked as the eyes of a clown.*
>
> *I was cryin ice cubes*
> *hoping I'd croak*
> *when the sun come through the window*
> *The ice all broke,*
> *I stood up and laughed*
> *thought it was a joke*
> *that's the way that the world goes round.*
> *You're up one day, the next you're down,*
> *It's a half an inch of water and you think you're gonna drown,*
> *That's the way that the world goes round.*
>
> —*John Prine*
> *"That's The Way That The World Goes Round"*

* * *

On June 4, at 30° 40' N, 152° 20' W, we found another Japanese fishing ball. On the tenth we spotted a California Grey Whale, headed south. On the fourteenth we finally hit the steady N'easterlies and a steady port tack, thanks to the famous North Pacific high pressure system.

On the seventeenth the batteries appeared dead. 450 miles from land. (We had been picking up commercial radio stations from the mainland—playing "Junkyard Dog," for instance. We had been out of touch with the world so long, the news we picked up astonished us, and we wondered what else had been going on? We felt like kids not invited to a birthday party—left out, wondering what we had missed.)

We got some crappy weather, as we expected when we approached land; thirty knot gusts, fifteen foot waves. We double-reefed until becalmed again on the nineteenth.

* * *

By the twentieth, still becalmed, 300 miles from the coast, and low on food, I seriously considered starting a routine of rowing toward shore. We felt so near, so far, after a terribly slow trip. It would be so ridiculous to get in trouble after coming so far, getting so close.

Suddenly, as I lay in my bunk, I started hearing things—voices. I knew there were no live radios on board. Everyone else below was asleep. The voices continued. Even concentrating to catch the words, I couldn't.

After about twenty minutes, Richard came down from watch, lay in his bunk for a few minutes, then asked if anyone was awake—yes—and did I hear anything strange, like voices—yes again, and goddam glad I'm not going wacko.

We listened for a while longer, then I went to the helm to ask Dan if he and Nancy had a radio. After I explained what was going on he said it sounded like the Bermuda Triangle to him. He would tell us about it tomorrow. The next day Dan described the Bermuda Triangle—a thousand-mile area in the Caribbean where ships and airplanes have mysteriously disappeared, compasses have gone berserk, and crazy unsolved mysteries still regularly occur. Theories vary. Simple coincidence? Magnetic disturbances? Some weird effects of the lost civilization of Atlantis?

Anyway the Bermuda Triangle wasn't our worry or our territory, and by then Richard and I had figured out the cause of the "voices": the internal halyards were vibrating inside the aluminum mast. The tension and wind must have been just right to create "human" sounds.

Some time after his albatross episode, the Ancient Mariner in Coleridge's poem heard spirit voices, too.

Thinking about the parallel, the Young Mariner decided to give in to fantasy, and "translate" what he heard:

First voice: Are we through punishing them for the death of Alby? Can we give "Orpheus" some wind now?

Second voice: Hell, no! Alby was one of my favorites.

First voice: But his death was an accident.

Second voice: Their fish hook did Alby in, and now they'll have to pay.

First voice: But all the crew were very sorry.

Second voice: Good. They're going to be sorrier.

First voice: Have you forgotten their Ti leaf?

Second voice: *Of course I haven't forgotten. Really? They have a Ti leaf? From Hawaii?*

First voice: *They have a Ti leaf from Hawaii.*

Second voice: *Oh, well, then, I suppose we'll have to let them have some wind. I wouldn't want to cross those Hawaiian spooks.*

First voice: *So "Orpheus" will reach shore.*

Second voice: *Undoubtedly. The leaf does that much for them. But there's no promise about what happens when they hit land, and I am still displeased with them.*

Sighting with the Plath sextant // Gentle sailing on the last leg home

17. a final good turn

In spite of the "voices," I expected an easy approach and landing at Ensenada.

Our navigation apprentice, Steve M., had been doing so well I hadn't even checked his charts for several days. This quiet, well-coordinated, unassuming man, who listened more than he talked, justified confidence. Whatever job you gave him he handled efficiently and effectively. I appreciated this kind of sailor—and friend.

His last LOP for the day put us about fifty miles due west of Ensenada. I glanced through the sailing directions, noting a twenty-two mile beacon, an eleven-mile beacon, and an island outside the bay. Nothing too exciting, with an early afternoon landfall.

Steve had wanted to try some moon sights and reductions, considering the ideal conditions of this last night at sea. A full moon rising after dark gave a good angle by ten p.m.

On this gorgeous night, enjoying the clear horizon, Steve practiced moon shots, and I took one, too. Our data checked, so we went below to reduce my results to the plotting chart. Steve watched as the LOP put us about two and a half miles west of Ensenada.

"Well, shit, I wonder what I did wrong," I said to myself as much as to Steve. "Must have made a math error." Though you couldn't trust or use moon shots in the early days of celestial navigation, the modern tables made the moon as useful as the sun and stars. But computation for moon sights differed a little from those of sun sights; and I hadn't done a moon sight reduction in several months. I was about halfway through the figures again when Richard hollered from the cockpit.

"Hey, Dick, we just sailed into a fog bank." I dropped the charts and flew up through the passageway, having to see for myself. "It just appeared from nowhere," Richard told me. We just numbly looked around for a few minutes, not comprehending the situation. DJ had warned me about a weather band fifty to one hundred miles off the coast, but had described it as rough seas and wind. I had had no personal experience in sailing off the mainland coast.

"I don't think it's anything to worry about. Probably just a band of crappy fog sitting off the coast. I'm glad we got that moon shot though."

Kiwi Steve stayed up on deck with Richard as an extra watch, and we turned on some lights and got the foghorn out. I got some comfort from Richard's assurance that the twenty-two mile beacon hadn't appeared.

I anxiously hurried back to the sight reduction, kicking myself for a lackadaisical indifference to our exact position. I had never before been encased in such thick fog at the time of landfall—and, strangely, to add to my sudden new worries, the wind had picked up to fifteen knots or so.

Suddenly Richard hollered again. Urgently. I got to the cockpit in a flash.

"It sounds like the surf!"

"It sure as hell does. Turn this son of a bitch around!"

We made a very fast about.

As we swung around I saw a beacon several hundred yards away. Our moon shot information had been all too accurate, and we had obviously arrived. We recovered from our shock as we sailed west a couple of miles.

"Hey, boys, we made it!"

"Yeah, that would have been one hell of an arrival, up on the rocks in Ensenada Bay."

"I wonder where the beacons were. Probably not working."

"Looks like you had the latitude just right, Steve."

"Fitting end to the voyage, I'd say." The last comment was from Richard, who summed it up quite well. We were all elated to be there, and our little navigation flub was not going to bring us down.

* * *

We hove-to off the coast until dawn, with a double watch, then sailed north to compensate for the current. The fog finally lifted about eleven a.m. We had been impatiently sailing inland at the time, with a bow watch ready at the anchor. Yellow quarantine flag flying, we glided in among the other yachts. A couple of people asked where we were coming in from. The answer, "New Zealand," left them blinking.

A sailor never forgets his good and bad moorings. In *The Lonely Sea and the Sky*, the great Chichester, for example, recalls his painful embarrassment at the end of one race, when his main halyard jammed at a crucial moment. The crew had just hooked onto a buoy—and with their boat still trying to sail, they had to hang on with brute force until Chichester finally got the main down. His colleagues had all seen the fiasco. In the clubhouse they slyly congratulated Chichester on "having the strongest crew in the club."

No such disaster for the *Orpheus* crew on our final mooring. The *Orpheus* came right up the breakwater with 165 jib and full main—the boaters staring in disbelief—and wormed through the moored vessels until we spotted our own place. A turn into the wind as the crew dropped the main—poof—just like that, tied to our mooring, and began getting shipshape. Damn, we were good!

* * *

The following chapter, 18, is meant to be a humorous view of the state Blue Orpheus ended up in. It is not intended in any way to be a slam on the boat, designer, engine manufacturer, sailmaker, or owner. On the contrary, I ended up with the highest regard for the boat. Of course I was fatigued and ready for land, and my journal reflected that. However, the engine's problem was its installation, not the motor itself. It was a miracle that any main sail could take the abuse we gave the Orpheus'. The boat and all its essential components kept us safe and alive. She was a good, strong boat that was supremely tested. In the preface of this book, I talked about the ancient elements. The element of water, particularly saltwater, can be corrosive as well as instructive. I will always be indebted to the Blue Orpheus for her strength and backbone. I will always be attached to her, and never forget the "umbilical cord" we had to the "Mother Ship."

18. welcome aboard, DJ!

Dan and Nancy **immediately disappeared.**
Sailors **they were** not.

The rest of us had a great time in bars that night, suffering no pangs of nostalgia about the sail coming to an end. I had been the only one to stay on board for the whole thing. That gave me a sense of pride, but I was worn out. So was the boat.

Stripping the boat in Ensenada

I had a vision of the way we could give DJ a tour of the *Orpheus*, and demonstrate the deterioration: DJ comes to visit, leans on the broken stern pulpit and falls in the drink. We throw him one of our two remaining floatable cushions, which promptly sinks. So we toss him instead a life preserver which has a leaky sea dye container, causing his clothing to be permanently stained. The crew quickly blows up the inflatable, forgetting its steady leaks, and as soon as DJ puts his weight on it it collapses. We are afraid to find out if our emergency raft will really inflate and work, so we fish him out with a boathook.

As he goes below he trips on the broken stairs and falls face first onto the floor, which is covered with foul bilge water because the manual bilge pump is broken and dead batteries leave the electric pumps inoperable.

We help him into the starboard upper bunk to recover,

but it collapses and he falls into the bilge water again. We would offer him dry clothing but ours is all rotten and moldy from sitting in bilge and sea water.

To warm himself he starts making coffee on the stove, which leaks fuel and

Getting towed to the pier in Ensenada

shoots out a two foot flame that won't stop. We offer him sardines and maggot-ridden flour and rice, which is all we have left. Meanwhile it begins raining and a steady drip from the leaky hatch covers slowly and thoroughly soaks him.

It is now dark but the lights won't go on because the batteries are dead and can't be charged because the engine won't run and the alternator is shot anyway.

Then, desiring a drink of water, he will have to haul out a rusty five gallon tin from the hatch, which contains some leavings that dated back to our Rarotonga stop. Getting sick from the "water" he will go for the head, slipping on diesel fuel from a leaky container kept in the cabin. As he falls he notices two big holes in the head door, caused by flying diesel cans. Disgusted, he goes up to raise the main and sail away. The main halyard breaks inside the mast, which it had been threatening to do for a couple of weeks. So there is no way he can use the main, which is just as well because it is a worn-out patchwork quilt.

Welcome aboard, DJ! The primary compass still works great.

Dad and me in Ensenada // With Mom on the "Orpheus" after the journey

Epilogue

My folks showed up the next day for a happy reunion. (My mother had had a vivid dream about me the night we made our scary landfall in the fog.)

They had letters from DJ instructing me to strip the boat and get everything to his friends' place in L.A. He listed about forty-five items, names, phone numbers, and a signed statement giving me the authority to transport the goods over the border.

The day after I did all that, I was met by the USCG, a banker, and a sheriff who all wanted to know what I was up to and if I was a business partner of DJ's. Once I convinced them I was not, which took several weeks, phone calls, and certified letters, the banker asked me if I would bring the boat up to the U.S. from Ensenada. I declined. There really wasn't enough of a boat left to sail or motor.

Years ago I ceased to take "phlogiston" seriously as a real element; the idea found a place on the same storage shelf where Santa Claus and other nice myths had already found a place a few years earlier. But at the very time I discarded the "reality," I found myself taking it all the more seriously as a symbol of something precious—"the true phlogiston" has become a synonym for me of "the superlative," including the best of human qualities.

In the testing process, and during my aging in saltwater, I came to recognize some new truths and experienced some basic reorientations. The most important, I think, was to witness the importance of ties to the rest of humanity. A soul has to have a connection with others to make sense. Experience and life alone are nothing more than a hollow bead among a dish of other beads—disjointed, crazy little isolated happenings. But put together with others, on a strong central thread, they make a necklace, a circle, a rich life, complete with the experience and love of other kindred souls.

In the South Pacific I found much more than the simple adventures I first expected. I found the way I hoped to continue living, with some adventures and risks to keep my system from "rusting out," some beautiful landscapes to let me sense the earth's movement in the galaxy, some music to touch one's soul, and some love to hold the meaning of existence together.

> *Keep not standing fix'd and rooted,*
> *Briskly venture, briskly roam!*
> *Head and hand, where'er thou foot it,*
> *And stout heart are still at home…*
> *To give space for wand'ring is it*
> *That the world was made so wide.*

—*Wilhelm Meister, Johann Wolfgang von Goethe*

APPENDIX—The Navigation Log (Partial)

11/24/72:	20° 30.0' N, 158° 05.0' W
11/25/72:	18° 17' N, 158° 55' W
11/26/72:	16° 19.0' N, 159° 15.1' W
11/27/72:	14° 00' N, 159° 22' W
11/28/72:	11° 35' N, 160° 03' W
11/29/72:	09° 00' N, 161° 04' W (169 miles)
11/30/72:	06° 24' N, 161° 48' W (161 miles)
12/1/72	5° 54' N, 162° 05' W
	Palmyra

12/5/72:	03° 46.5' N, 163° 18.5' W
12/6/72:	01° 50' N, 163° 27' W
12/7/72:	0° 30' S, 164° 40' W (139 miles)
12/8/72:	02° 13' S, 165° 28.1' W (112 miles)
12/9/72:	04° 24' S, 166° 22' W (139 miles)
12/10/72:	05° 23.1' S, 166° 45.8' W (60 miles)
12/11/72:	07° 25' S, 167°13' W (122 miles)
12/12/72:	09° 23' S, 168°10.1' W (132 miles)
12/1372:	11° 33' S, 168° 53.5' W (135 miles)
12/14/72:	13° 05' S, 169° 50' W (110 miles)
	American Samoa

12/22/72:	17° 09' S, 172° 40' W
	Va Va'U

12/29/72:	19° 02' S, 174° 25' W
	Tonga

1/5/73:   22° 52' S, 175° 32' W
1/6/73:   24° 19' S, 176° 27' W
1/7/73:   26° 07' S, 177° 37' W (127 miles)
1/8/73:   27° 53' S, 179° 05' W (132 miles)
1/9/73:   29° 47' S, 179° 38' E
              (148 miles—International Date Line)
1/10/73:   32° 02' S, 178° 29' E (145 miles)
1/11/73:   33° 35' S, 177° 27' E (105 miles)
1/12/73:   34° 46' S, 176° 37' E (83 miles)
1/13/73:   35° 00' S, 176° 00' E (estimate)
1/14/73:   Auckland, New Zealand

2/22/73:   35° 24' S, 178° 12' E
2/23/73:   34° 13' S, 178° 50' W
              (165 miles—International Date Line)
2/24/73:   32° 55' S, 176° 42' W (135 miles)
2/25/73:   31° 12' S, 174° 08' W
2/26/73:   28° 20' S, 171° 40' W (60 miles)
2/27/73   27° 00' S, 170° 20' W (100 miles)
2/28/73:   25° 48' S, 169° 00' W (100 miles)
2/29–3/5:   No reliable sights due to storm
3/5/73:   21° 11' S, 162° 25' W (92 miles)
3/6/73:   21° 00' S, 160° 32' W (40 miles to go)
3/7/73:   Rarotonga

3/16/73:   21° 00' S, 156° 55' W (165 miles)
3/17/73:   21° 07' S, 155° 23' W (87 miles)
3/18/73:   20° 10' S, 154° 50' W (75 miles)
3/19/73:   19° 08' S, 153° 30' W (95 miles)
3/20/73:   18° 30' S, 152° 03' W (86 miles)
              The Society Islands

4/25/73:	12° 47' S, 152° 15' W (230 miles)
4/26/73:	10° 40' S, 152° 36' W (127 miles)
4/27/73:	09° 42' S, 153° 45' W (90 miles)
4/28/73:	07° 18' S, 154° 56' W (162 miles)
4/29/73:	05° 29' S, 155° 36' W (108 miles)
4/30/73:	03° 19' S, 156° 36' W (144 miles)
5/1/73:	01° 28' S, 157° 12' W (120 miles)
5/2/73:	00° 07' S, 157° 18' W (85 miles)
5/3/73:	**Christmas Island**

5/7/73:	04° 41' N, 156° 47' W
5/8/73:	07° 20' N, 156° 59' W (159 miles)
5/9/73:	09° 06' N, 157° 31' W (110 miles)
5/10/73:	10° 51' N, 157° 37' W (105 miles)
5/11/73	12° 38' N, 157° 29' W (107 miles)
5/12/73:	14° 00' N, 157° 20' W (82 miles)
5/13/73:	15° 22' N, 157° 14' W (79 miles)
5/14/73:	17° 04' N, 156° 57' W (104 miles)
5/15/73:	**Hilo**

5/30/73:	22° 35' N, 153° 54' W (188 miles)
5/31/73:	24° 52' N, 153° 35' W (138 miles)
6/1/73:	27° 20' N, 153° 15' W (150 miles)
6/4/73:	30° 40' N, 152° 20' W (37 miles)
6/5/73:	30° 39' N, 151° 25' W (47 miles)
6/6/73:	31° 06' N, 150° 57' W (37 miles)
6/7/73:	31° 55' N, 148° 40' W (100 miles)
6/8/73:	33° 20' N, 144° 29' W (94 miles)
6/17/73:	33° 05' N, 127° 40' W
6/19/73:	32° 42' N, 121° 42' W (150 miles)
6/22/73:	**Ensenada**

Stealing Nam Sang

Based Upon a True Story

Richard (DJ) Johnson

photo credit: Warren Roll, Bishop Museum (www.bishopmuseum.org)

Nam Sang winning the Transpac Yacht Race, 1957, Diamond Head, Hawaii

Preface

photo credit: Jack Hickson; State Library of NSW, Sydney, Australia

Richard "DJ" Johnson and I met again almost forty years after my voyage in the "Blue Orpheus." The following are some of his notes regarding his adventures with "Nam Sang," and they speak for themselves in regard to this amazing individual. I am proud to include them as a mini-sequel to "Aged in Saltwater."

—RKW

Nam Sang winning the 1961 Hobart Yacht Race, Australia

"*Stealing Nam Sang*" is based upon a true story about the famous and/or infamous beautiful 72' racing sailboat, written by the owner, Richard Johnson, an experienced sailor, marine navigator, and ex-airline captain. The author uses the term "stolen" out of New Zealand as accused and by sailing her out by himself to the first United States possession where the United States Coast Guard could determine the rightful ownership. Otherwise, according to a U.S. Maritime Attorney's personal experience, claimants would come out of the woodwork and would prevent *Nam Sang* from ever leaving New Zealand. It was discreetly mentioned that only "self help" would get her out of New Zealand.

This story begins by leading up to why and how *Nam Sang* was on a voyage from the Long Beach Yacht Club to Auckland, New Zealand in the first place. It explains that four escaping felony drug fugitives turned out to be part of the "crew" and took control of *Nam Sang* as soon as they were at sea and learned a little about how to sail her. The author was not aboard *Nam Sang* on this voyage, but has interviewed crew members of the "ship of fools" who, by some miracle, made it to within 500 miles of New Zealand before being dismasted. An armed mutiny by the drugged cowards prevented the experienced sailors from reefing the mainsail and lowering the large genoa headsail before an approaching storm and not after the storm hit.

After two days of gale force winds and heavy seas, and still under full sails, the mast finally went overboard along with the sails and rigging.

The second these fugitives stepped off *Nam Sang* in Auckland they were interviewed by the *New Zealand Herald Press* and began their drummed up heroic nonsense about how they saved *Nam Sang*. Within days they got the drug business going, stole everything they could possibly remove from the boat, and figured out how to forge *Nam Sang's* documents and fraudulently tried to sell her. In a short time they were back in jail and deported to the U.S.

This background makes interesting reading, but the unbelievable and fascinating story begins after the author finally found *Nam Sang* after almost 20 years during which time *Nam Sang* was reportedly running drugs from Southeast Asia, with the "owners" taking out fraudulent loans, bankruptcies, and avoiding DEA.

Read how the author, by some miracle, was able to sail a 100,000 pound 72-foot cutter with an 86-foot overall mast and 24-foot boom with huge sails (that were normally raced with a 16–18 person crew) out of New Zealand and above all, how he did it alone with no help from anyone in New Zealand. The story vividly explains the reasoning and legality for "escaping" or "retrieving" in this dangerous manner compared to how *Nam Sang* was accursedly "stolen", as reported in a June 1993 *New Zealand Herald* article, and sailed out of New Zealand by some crew. You won't believe the differences in these two stories.

```
-One-
```
SPECIAL LOVE

Unique Special Love

There is something different that a sailor has for his boat. The affection for a sailboat is something like the love for a child. It isn't a "normal" relationship, like owning a piece of personal or real property. I am not talking about a skiff or day sailor, but an offshore ocean-going sailboat. Something that, when all else fails, you can get aboard and sail off to anywhere in the world. Get away from everything and everybody. It's more than just a home; it's a complete change of life the second you decide you have had enough of what's happening, and it becomes your ticket to a new world and life. It is like a security blanket, or an insurance policy towards a free and better existence. You can go to any marina and see all the sailboats just sitting there with no one around, no activity, no usage, and wonder why the owners are paying $300 per month mooring along with all the taxes, insurance, upkeep etc. The answer is just exactly what I am talking about. It's that special feeling and security that when the shit hits the fan, they can be off!! It's not because they want to tell everyone that they "own a yacht" (and they don't!); rather it's because they love this thing and love the lifestyle it can bring the second they decide to go.

In my case I actually loved the boat I didn't have from the time I was about 12 years old. I read every book I could find about sailing and especially "sailing around the world", such as the Joshua Slocum voyages. I would ride my bike or hitchhike 15 miles to the San Pedro or Wilmington boat yard and sneak aboard sailboats on the "hard". Then my favorite was a 60-some foot beautifully designed and built wooden boat from Germany. It looked like it had been there for years and the planking seams were open, but I loved this boat and knew I could fix her even though I knew it would never happen. That didn't matter, as I knew I would have something like her someday. I must have ridden back and forth from my home 15 times when I was 12 years old to this boat, just dreaming of the day. By the time I was 14 years old I am sure I had been to every marina from Newport Beach to Marina Del Rey. I hadn't sailed 10 feet but I knew most every sailboat in the marinas and boat yards and read over 100 books on sailing and voyages/ports in the world. I really had it bad! I didn't want to have the indecision and boring future my friends seemed to have, but I had the desire to do something exciting and different. The only way I knew how, at this time, was sailing in my own boat anywhere in the world I wanted to go.

- Two -
MY NAM SANG HISTORY

Nam Sang was one of the boats I would ride my bike 15 miles to see when I was only 14. She was in Newport Beach and beautiful. I was never aboard, but it was love at first sight. My good friend Don Canfield actually worked on her, mostly diving to clean her bottom and varnishing her bright work, but he did meet some of the movie stars on board and cleaned up after them.

Through the years I had followed *Nam Sang's* racing
career and famous owners. During one summer at college,
I worked as a waiter at the beautiful five-star restaurant
casino at Avalon, Catalina Island. After work at night we
would ride around in the water taxi picking up and taking
crew members and guests back to their boats. *Nam Sang*
was often in the harbor in the best mooring in front of
the Marlin Club. She was owned by Paramount Studios
and Ray Milan and there was always some party going on!
Most of the action was below with lights, music, laughing,
screaming, and moaning, but occasionally some beautiful
thing would come above deck for air or whatever. Oh how
my friends and I would have loved to be a part of these
parties. For me it just added to my addiction to sailing
and I knew it would be on some beautiful sailboat like the
famous *Nam Sang*.

I saw her again years later when I had a layover in Honolulu.
By this time I was a copilot flying internationally (aviation
was my second love).

Nam Sang had just won the most prestigious sailing race in
the world, the Transpac Race from San Pedro to Honolulu,
and was being outfitted for return to San Francisco. What a
beautiful sight. She was on "mahogany row" at the Hawaii
Yacht Club guest slip among the most beautiful sailboats
in the world. No one was aboard but I could just sit on the
dock and dream. I do not believe in supernatural events,
but what happened next could make one wonder.

-Three-
LEADING UP TO BUYING NAM SANG

My plan in 1972 was to build a 70-foot fast offshore race sailboat that would also have spartan crew quarters for up to 14 crew members, designed by an excellent race designer from New Zealand. Dick Williams, who sailed the *Blue Orpheus* with me to New Zealand, was sailing her back from New Zealand with a crew from New Zealand while I was building another bigger boat. Then I met the owner of *San Souci* at the Long Beach Yacht Club and he asked me if I would like to buy her. I said no to the buying part but would be interested in leasing her while I built my own 70' sailboat. The owner said sure and told me to take her for a couple of weeks; if I liked her we could work out the lease amount and just pay the slip fees during the time I had her.

San Souci (without care) was a 110-foot sloop/cutter made in Australia. She was fast, strong, had nice quarters, and a big auxiliary engine. I made some shake-down sails to Catalina Island with my experienced sailing friends, working out any rigging, sails, or other handling problems, and made the decision she was more than capable of sailing to New Zealand or most anywhere, as *San Souci* was a strong, fast seaworthy sailboat. We worked out a simple month-to-month lease agreement and I took possession of *San Souci.*

"Sailing to New Zealand
Join Crew!"

Hundreds of people answered my two line ad in the *L.A. Times,* wanting to do exactly what I liked to do, which was have some excitement, fun, and travel. It was easy for me to describe what sailing to New Zealand was like because I had just sailed to New Zealand in the *Blue Orpheus,* an Ericson 39, from Hawaii, and had as much fun in New Zealand as a person could have with such friendly, beautiful girls, parties, countryside, beaches, marinas, and about every other thing you could hope for. In addition, this "share the expense" cost wouldn't be any more than flying to New Zealand. The trade of time for adventure was an easy decision for the type of person who answered my ad. As might be expected, only a very few knew how to sail, and actually most had never been on a sailboat.

I had enough experience with crew who had never sailed before and would be able to honestly describe the distinct possibility of really bad seasickness, boredom, discomfort, danger, close quarters, rough seas, a 90% chance that they would absolutely hate sailing, and about every other thing I could think of. Most were young and said this is exactly what they were looking for! There were some who really wanted to go but who I turned down because of the physical demands of a long strenuous voyage. We had one really experienced sailor and crew member who had crewed for me in the 1971 Transpac Race to Honolulu. John wanted to go with me on the sail to New Zealand and I was delighted to have him as "first mate." He would be fully capable of being the master or captain if I was not able for some physical or other problem. John also helped me in determining the fitness of potential crew members.

It seemed that most were the "backpacker" type of girls and guys, and in my mind, a perfect fit for offshore sailing—strong, in good physical shape, rugged and compatible, fun people to be around. John and I selected 15 people—4 girls and 11 guys.

Four of the crew were the Maestries—Michael and his wife Peggy, Michael's brother Peter and their business partner. They were from the Midwest somewhere. Since they were all together, it seemed having a good percentage of the crew as friends was a benefit to all the crew members.

-Four-
MY FIRST "STEALING" NAM SANG

The most incredible thing happened while we moved *San Souci* from the guest slip at Long Beach Yacht Club to a slip in the San Pedro marina, where we were interviewing potential crew members, having fun, and preparing to leave in a few days for New Zealand. *Nam Sang* was towed in by the Harbor Police, escorted by the USCG to the empty slip right next to ours. On board *Nam Sang* were at least one dozen uniformed and plainclothes men with guns and at least one big black shepherd dog. There didn't seem to be anyone on board who was arrested but *Nam Sang* was certainly under police, DEA, customs and/or USCG control, as well as a half-dozen uniformed and dozen plainclothes serious-looking men and women who looked like they all had weapons under or outside their clothes.

They promptly installed the customary yellow danger warning banner.

We were in talking distance to the guys on *Nam Sang* and they were all friendly to us and more than happy to give us the story of what was going down. There were many rumors that *Nam Sang* had been involved in drugs in some way for years. They caught *Nam Sang* as she was leaving Newport Beach and approximately 20 miles off shore, heading south with about a dozen persons on board. These officers all said the owner of the boat had nothing to do with the operation of this sailboat and had done everything he could for years to repossess her, as well as keeping the DEA informed of *Nam Sang's* track and ports of call.

The officers on *Nam Sang* told me that as soon as they completed their search for drugs and other evidence they would immediately turn *Nam Sang* over to the USCG documented owner's possession and would have no further involvement with this vessel and that *Nam Sang* was not confiscated.

It took me about one hour to get to the USCG documentation office in Long Beach to find the owner's name. All I had to do was have the name of the boat and they would be happy to give the present owner's name as they had computer records. In a few minutes I was given the information and it only took another 30 minutes to go to the owner's place of business in Torrance, California, learning all I could about the boat I had admired for almost my whole adult life, the beautiful *Nam Sang*. Mr. Thompson

was the president of a very successful business and only
20 minutes from the marina. I went to his office with the
intention of being as nice as I could to someone who just got
his boat confiscated. I didn't know what to expect when I got
to the office, but it went something like this:

I told the receptionist that "I would like to speak to Mr.
Thompson for a moment" and I heard on the speaker,
"What about?"

I yelled, "*Nam Sang*".

"What about *Nam Sang*?"

"Please let me just ask you something!"

"OK, just for a minute," and I was ushered in, saying hello to
a real nice looking guy who didn't want to shake my hand.

"What do you want?"

"I want to talk to you about *Nam Sang*."

Thompson said "I DON'T WANT TO TALK ABOUT
Nam Sang!, PERIOD!" and as quick as I could get it out of
my mouth I said,

"I don't want to talk either, I wanted to buy *Nam Sang*, for
cash, how much do you want for her?"

Thompson said "_____dollars, cash, as is!"

I said "Okay. I will be back in less than an hour". This whole "negotiation" took less than five minutes and I was out of the office for a total of about 10 minutes.

I called my best friend Earl Waggoner, who lived in Manhattan Beach, to loan me the cash and meet me at Thompson's office immediately. Earl had just made captain with TWA and had all kinds of money and had been helping me get ready to sail on *San Souci*. He had also introduced me to a beautiful girl who was going with me to New Zealand and was now staying with Earl while we were getting ready to leave. I went to my friendly banker in Long Beach and got my cash and met Earl in front of Thompson's office. Earl had checked with his banker friend and found Thompson's company was a very reputable and successful firm, so neither Earl or I had any presumption of an illicit fraudulent transaction, even though we would have much preferred to have given Thompson a cashier's check. I went in alone, ushered into Thompson's office, and presented the cash.

We wrote up a simple bill of sale which would be all I would need, along with my U.S. passport, to enable me to get the USCG documentation transferred.

I just "stole" *Nam Sang*! However, in this case it was not literally but figuratively "a bargain," as what I paid Thompson for *Nam Sang* was, in my mind, a steal. Thompson had spent hundreds of thousands on *Nam Sang*, including the cost of dismasting off the coast of New Zealand, a new mast, rigging, sails and buying her in the first place. We were to become friends and he never said a word about his side of the bargain, later giving me moral support in what was to happen to me in New Zealand.

But right now, in Thompson's office, for the first time I saw a ray of likability in Thompson. In fact, he was almost friendly, so I asked him if he wouldn't come down to *Nam Sang* with me so I could look below just in case there was any question of the right to be aboard. Thompson said, "Here we go—this was an as-is transaction!" I responded as quickly as I could that I only wanted to take a quick look inside and had no intention of complaining about anything. Nor did I really care if anything was below deck, I was just happy to be able to buy the boat I had loved for a long, long time. Thompson, actually being a real nice guy, understood and agreed, as it was only a few miles away and before the traffic would pick up, but only for a second. And off we went in his nice Cadillac. We were about one mile from the marina, when he pulled over and said, "I can't do it." We turned around and headed back to his office where he sadly explained how he felt and how much he had loved *Nam Sang*. Some of the happiest years of his life were spent owning and sailing *Nam Sang,* including sailing to Australia and the Sidney Hobart Race. There was also the nightmare of trying to catch these bunch of s.o.b. druggies these last two years. To this day, I fully appreciate and understand the way he felt, as I was about to experience almost the same thing.

-Five-
NAM SANG TO NEW ZEALAND

Switching from *San Souci* to *Nam Sang*

All of our "crew" was really happy to be changing boats from *San Souci* to *Nam Sang,* because even though *San Souci* was a little larger, there was just something about *Nam Sang* that drew you to her—wanting to be aboard and, above all, go sailing aboard her. The trouble was, we had to take four less crew members because of the smaller size, and I asked if any of the 16 would want to volunteer to not go on this voyage. Donna had fallen in love with Earl, the good-looking airline captain with three Ferraris to upstage her new yellow Jaguar convertible, so we were down to three. We had two reluctant volunteers and now had to select one more crew. I decided, along with a couple others, who the person would be. There was something about this guy that wasn't particularly likable and we were soon to find out why. He said either he was going or none of us were going and stormed off. Wow! What kind of a nut was this guy?

The crew was pretty green. Three had a lot of good sailing backgrounds and one was a perfect "first mate" who had extensive experience. There were four who had probably never seen the ocean before coming out here and certainly didn't have any sailing experience, but all seemed like nice people and very anxious to come. They were rather fun to be with and even stayed with Kathy, Karen Mashburn, and me at Karen's house in Belmont Shore for a week while we prepared *Nam Sang* for the trip. I thought this would be a good idea because the married couple could stay in the main stateroom which was the only quarters that had a double bunk.

There was nothing really unusual about this foursome while they were staying with us. I know they had some joints but were never wasted and never smoked in the house. I had made it perfectly clear about smoking, both cigarettes and dope especially on board *Nam Sang*. There aren't many things dumber than having dope aboard a sailing vessel, especially when at sea and arriving in a foreign port like New Zealand. I never heard more "oh yes we certainly understand and would never do such a crazy thing." Kathy, Karen, and I had certainly been around enough, though, that we could pick up on someone with drug problems and the last thing we thought was any drug problems with these nice Midwestern farmer-type folk.

We were all loaded and motored over to the Long Beach Yacht Club where I was a member and did the final preparations at the guest dock, as we were to clear out with the USCG for the sail to New Zealand. I had lived in Belmont Shore, Long Beach, most of my life and I think about everyone I knew was going to be at our going away party at LBYC. No doubt this was going to a fun, huge sendoff!

The afternoon before our sendoff party at the club, a USCG office told me that I could not go as this voyage has "paying passengers" even though they are only "sharing the expense" of the trip. This officer had a big book of USCG regulations and presented me with the exact regulation as legal authority. I had previously invited an inspection of the safety requirements on board *Nam Sang* which they gave me, checked off a checklist of items, and there was certainly nothing missing, safety-wise. However, as the Coast Guard Officer now explained, crew sharing the expense of a voyage is certainly legal but the vessel owner cannot be on board either as the captain/master or guest. Since I now owned *Nam Sang,* there was no way I could go on this sail to New Zealand or anywhere else. Period!

This was certainly a disappointing setback for me, but no real problem as I would have John take over to be the "Sailing Master." John was an experienced big boat crewman and had sailed on the Transpac Race with me. He was an experienced celestial navigator and had a background that was well prepared to skipper *Nam Sang* on this sail. There was only one stop on the way, which was Pago Pago in American Samoa. This was a sail to New Zealand, not a South Pacific Island visit. I would just fly to New Zealand and meet *Nam Sang* when she arrived in a little over a month. So we still had the going-away party and off *Nam Sang* went to New Zealand the morning after the party, sans me.

I gave the Maestries my ham radio call sign and explained how to do a telephone patch to my telephone number at Kathy's. But, since they were not licensed, I urged them to not use the ham unless it was an emergency. The skipper, John, was licensed by the FCC to use the marine single sideband radio which would enable them to give the USCG their position in case of an emergency. None of us ever heard from any of them by radio or any other way of communication. Absolutely nothing!

I did get a call from Dick Williams, who was bringing *Blue Orpheus* back from New Zealand for me. He said *Nam Sang* had just left Hilo a few days earlier. This was really strange because it was a simple downwind sail from Long Beach to Hilo, which should take no more than 20 days maximum and they had taken over a month!

I was to later find out why. John, the skipper, got deathly ill about a week after leaving Long Beach and had to go to the nearest port, Hilo. Why he didn't call me or have someone call me I'll never know, as I could have flown over the day I found out and either taken over *Nam Sang* or found someone who was capable of skippering from Hilo to New Zealand. Had I known then what was going on aboard *Nam Sang* I would have prevented her from moving out of the slip, never leaving Hilo. But she was gone and left days before I even knew she had arrived.

I wasn't aboard *Nam Sang* so I don't have any firsthand way of describing this ship of mostly fools and a couple of real heroes who told me their unbelievable story after leaving Hilo. The hero's hero was Kerch, a top-notch sailor and now a USCG licensed master of both sail and power. Kerch promised me he was going to write or actually finish writing a book about the sail to hell along with the pictures of these Maestries and the other cowardly drug addicts.

But here is what I do know. All three of the Maestries and some others were felony fugitives from the United States. Now I knew why they were so excited to be going with us to New Zealand. They would never be able to get on a plane out of the USA. What a perfect way to avoid capture, just sail away and arrive in New Zealand as crew members. They were not picked up in Hilo because they were simply traveling from one state to another with no custom or immigration entry required. I do know that the DEA wanted to board *Nam Sang* (for drugs, not the felons), but were not allowed aboard without a search warrant. It wasn't these guys "first time on the beach" so to speak and they were out of Hilo before any more searches occurred. I was dumb and happy about all of this, waiting in Australia for *Nam Sang* to arrive in New Zealand.

I eventually got a call from Kathy Mashburn, telling me to call Don East in New Zealand and that *Nam Sang*, although safely in Auckland, had been dismasted. I called Don and got most of the dismasting story about these druggies—what cowards they were by not having the nerve to lower sails in a moderate storm, how they threatened to kill anyone who did and waved around a couple of pistols. Could I believe all of this? I was in a state of shock, but as I look back now, what a miracle no one was hurt except *Nam Sang.* Even she motored into Auckland safely, sans mast, rigging and sails.

I flew over to Auckland on the next flight I could find to check out *Nam Sang* and to learn all I could about what happened. When I got to Auckland the next day it was a sickening sight but something that I had witnessed before—being dismasted during a race and what it takes to repair the damage, which is time and money. *Nam Sang* had some hull work and stanchion damage but not much more. I didn't want to waste any time getting *Nam Sang* repaired in New Zealand since I didn't know a place in Auckland that had the facilities and experience to make a new mast and rigging. From what I know now, Auckland would have been the perfect location to make all the mast and rigging repairs. At this time, I made arrangements for the *Nam Sang* to be towed or driven from the government docks to a marina and I went back to the U.S. to build or buy a mast and rigging. I knew of a mast and rigging in Newport Beach that I could buy and ship to New Zealand, which was actually a perfect height and with excellent standing rigging. All I would need was to make arrangements to ship the mast to New Zealand. It was off a boat that had been hijacked in Honolulu and damaged a little during the recovery. but the owners had demanded a new mast. This was a perfect mast for *Nam Sang* and a fast, not-too-expensive repair.

It took me more than two weeks to arrange buying and shipping the mast to New Zealand and while this work was being done, I flew back to Auckland to arrange things on the New Zealand end. After I finally found *Nam Sang's* location, I couldn't believe what I saw. My beautiful *Nam Sang* had been stripped of everything that could be stolen, including all the winches, unique stanchions, remaining sails, plaques, tools, radios, instruments, galley stove, engine accessories, etc. There wasn't much left but a bare hull and the engine and prop that they probably couldn't figure out to get out or off. I couldn't believe what I saw, my beautiful *Nam Sang* now out of the water in some cradle in some boat yard.

At this time I had enough of New Zealand and the type of seafaring people who would do this kind of thing. I got the first flight I could out of this place to retrun home, where I could grasp what had happened. There wasn't a thing I could do about *Nam Sang* right now as I had only enough money to fly home.

On the flight home I realized all the good things. I had a beautiful girlfriend Kathy and an Airline Pilots rating, although no airline jobs because of no fuel with the Arab mess. I could manufacture Kamados again and make money even though there was nothing exciting about making and selling anything, especially something that I had already successfully done. But if you could do it once, you could do it again, as some useless story goes.

-Six-
FIRST ATTEMPT

After a few years flying the Electra, a four engine propjet, taking passengers from all over the country to a Lake Havasu land development, I thought I had made enough money to get *Nam Sang* home. I went back to New Zealand to see if I could figure out how to get *Nam Sang* out of this place. She was in Whangarei sitting in the small marina on dry land for all this time. The hull was dried out and required caulking, but other than that everything was the same as I had left it a couple years ago. I knew how to caulk the hull and set about caulking the entire 70 foot hull myself. In about a week I had this caulking somewhat near the finish and called my friend George Adams to see if he wanted to come over and help finish caulking. We could get some jury rig mast and sail *Nam Sang* home. George had sailed with me on the Transpac Race from Los Angeles to Honolulu on my Ericson 39 and we had won a few big races together. George's girlfriend, Karen Mashburn, and my girlfriend Kathy were sisters. George was the biggest, toughest guy I knew, along with being a great friend and sailor. As expected, George said he would be right over if I promised some excitement, as he was bored with nothing going on around his place.

After George came over to New Zealand, we somehow got *Nam Sang* into the water with the help of some of the nicest and talented movers you could ever meet. They used tractors and winches to somehow get *Nam Sang* about 100 yards and into the water. To this day, I don't see how they moved a 100,000 pound boat without a crane but they did. I started the engine after all these years and she ran fine. I had bought a 50-foot electric wooden pole that we would hoist aboard for a jury rig and a used sail and some rigging. Our plans were to motor down the Whangarei waterway to the bay and anchor while we completed the jury rig and got supplies. I had a rental car back at the boat to use for picking up fuel and supplies. No one had even asked what we were doing working on *Nam Sang* or why or what we were going to do.

While I was in Auckland picking up stuff, George was boarded by about four guys and a couple of Doberman pinchers while at anchor in the bay. George was more than capable of throwing them off *Nam Sang* but the dogs and the possibility of them having guns made his decision both hard and easy. When I hailed George on *Nam Sang* from the shore, he said he had company and described the situation. They took George ashore and that was the end of our failed attempt. Somehow we both got home. I had a friend wire me a ticket and George somehow got home, although the New Zealand police arrested him for stealing a dingy (or some other reason), but released him in a few hours. The whole scene was bad, sad and whatever other nightmare you could think of.

My New Zealand girlfriend gave me the money to buy a ticket to LAX and I had no other trouble. George, on the other hand, had a nightmare getting out and home.

In a few days, both George and I were back at our girlfriends' house, licking our wounds and wondering what was next. While we were watching the 11 pm news and having our second six pack, a special announcement came on KCLA that there was an urgent request for C130 pilots to fly the critical Cambodian airlift out of the Phnom Penh seige and to immediately call some 800 number. Since I was still sober enough to call, I got a simple, "Do you have a passport and can you leave immediately?" I responded,

"Yes, of course," and without ever asking if I knew how to fly a C130, the operator requested that I meet some colonel at the Thai embassy at ten in the morning. I hadn't the slightest idea what I was doing nor I am sure did they, but I was broke and this was a job, I hoped. I was at the Thai embassy promptly at 10 am and asked for the colonel. The clerk said she was expecting me and asked for my passport. In a few minutes she returned with my passport and an envelope with a ticket the next day for Tokyo, another ticket to Bangkok, Thailand, a membership to the officers club in Bangkok, and a wad of cash. I thought, "Hey, this is great and so far, so good, especially with the one-thousand dollars in the envelope." The passport was a visa for Richard Johnson working for Thai Rock Products. There was only one little problem now—I had never flown a C130 or even been in one! But, while with American Airlines I did get a rating for a L188 (Lockheed Electra), which had exactly the same engines and cockpit as the C130. I figured I could wing it, especially since my nephew was stationed in a reserve C130 unit in Van Nuys and could get me a USAF flight manual. This would give me most of what I needed to fly the thing.

To make a long, unbelievable story short, I did pass my AF C130H check ride at Utapao Air Force Base, the most secretive Air Force base in the world. One "mission" check later and I was on my own flying some of the most incredible flights you could ever imagine flying into Phnom Penh, this crazy besieged place. We were paid by the "mission", and more money than I could ever imagine. Before I was "shot" out of my job, I had thousands of "tax-free" CIA dollars and thousands more after I got home, magically appearing in the mail.

All of this CIA stuff is only applicable to *"Stealing Nam Sang"*—raising the money and figuring out how to accomplish my goal of getting *Nam Sang* out of New Zealand. There wasn't a day that I didn't think about *Nam Sang* and how much I was pissed about the whole New Zealand episode. Now I had plenty of money to go to New Zealand and do whatever it took to get *Nam Sang* out of that place.

There was a little problem, though—I couldn't find out where she was!

-Seven-
WE FOUND NAM SANG

At our New Year's party George and I were discussing what really pissed us off the most. We both agreed it was our failure to get *Nam Sang* out of New Zealand after all the work—getting her out of that boat yard, out to the bay of Whangarei, ready to sail/motor/float or whatever to get her to international waters and away from these nuts. Then, with success about to make it, failed! We never got *Nam Sang* out of New Zealand or anywhere else.

We both remembered that John Allenby was sailing around the world. Hugh Brady had his telephone number, thinking he was still in New Zealand on his yacht and actually doing some work in Auckland.

The next day, Sunday, I called John and learned that he actually spent New Year's in the Bay of Islands and *Nam Sang* was anchored near a few boats. They had a few drinks aboard with some people that said they owned *Nam Sang*. John didn't remember their names, but said they owned a slip in Bay Harbor Marina. He hadn't done a survey or looked closely at her condition, but thought she was seaworthy, at least from all the stories they had been telling them. He thought they wanted to sell *Nam Sang* but had no other details. I thanked John very much but did not go into anything about my history with *Nam Sang* or any of my thoughts at the time. I knew John had some business relationship with a New Zealand company and an English Company called Ellenby's, plus he had his beautiful yacht in Auckland. I did not want to get him involved with anything that I might be planning in New Zealand, other than learning *Nam Sang's* location. I would have liked his help in New Zealand, but for some reason it didn't seem John was the right one since I hardly knew him other than a few social dinners at Hugh Brady's beautiful house in Point Arena, California.

This unexpected surprise of finding where *Nam Sang* actually was put me in a whole different mental approach toward my goals. Clearly, the first step would be to go to New Zealand and check out the scene for myself before making a big life-changing decision to leave a nice successful, yet boring, business, home, family and all the routine daily life! Even if I were able to bring *Nam Sang* back, owning a big sailboat is actually a lifestyle change from living in Sacramento. On the other hand, I could always get her back to San Francisco or Newport Beach and sell her for at least a few hundred thousand dollars or more, depending on her condition, since *Nam Sang* was a famous boat. Selling *Nam Sang* would make good "business sense" but not to me; I wanted *Nam Sang* back, period! I have always had that kind of weird "boat love" that only sailboat owners can really feel, and making money selling your boat isn't part of it.

In less than 48 hours I was on a plane to Auckland, New Zealand. I rented a car and drove directly to Bay Harbor Marina—a beautiful marina only a few minutes from downtown Auckland. The marina had nice facilities, boat repair, sail makers, marine supplies and is near a nice town with repair shops, auto stores, etc. One good thing was there were no gates to the slips like there are on virtually all marinas in the USA.

I didn't have to ask anyone where *Nam Sang* was because she was the biggest boat in the marina and on an end slip, so all I did was walk down to see if anyone was aboard. There was no one on her or any of the boats nearby. After pounding on the hull, I took my shoes off—the first indication of a sailor—climbed aboard and just sat there… here I am aboard *Nam Sang!* I guess I was in the first stage of boat happiness, whatever that is. After 30 minutes of this trance, I looked at every inch of the hull, deck, mast, rigging, winches, windless; everything looked fine.

There was a GPS receiver and some cockpit instruments, nothing special that would be required for racing but enough for normal cruising, mainly a knot meter, wind speed and direction.   All the engine instruments were below in the navigation/engine aft cabin. What I was most concerned about, from a time and money standpoint, was the condition of the huge mainsail which was furled on the boom under a nice sail cover. I took most of the sail cover off and inspected the main the best I could and in my opinion, the sail was well-made from heavy modern Dacron and triple-seamed nicely. Overall I would say about an 85% or more quality main; really good news! From what I could see below through the port holes and sky lights (as all hatches were locked) all looked fine and there were a couple of marine radios. Below the waterline, it looked like all the bottom really needed was just a bottom dive cleaning job and future need of anti-fouling paint, but it was not necessary to haul her at this time. It didn't look like this marina had anything that could haul a deep-keeled sailboat this size, but Auckland certainly did have equipment if it were necessary to take her out of the water. I could dive and do any of the other repairs like changing the strut bearings, prop, etc.

Overall, in about two hours of uninterrupted time on my *Nam Sang* survey, I concluded that it wouldn't take me more than a week or two to prepare *Nam Sang* for a trip home. One exception was the condition of the auxiliary engine and transmission and if it would even run or go into gear. But, if either the transmission or engine needed repair, Auckland would be as good a place to have the work done right and as inexpensive a place as anywhere in the world. This problem wouldn't stop getting *Nam Sang* home, it would just take more time.

In less than two days I found out what I came to New Zealand to determine: is *Nam Sang* seaworthy enough to get her at least out of New Zealand? Absolutely! Now, I would go home and figure out HOW. I did not meet or talk to anyone about *Nam Sang* as I would first figure out my plan before I met or discussed anything with the ship's broker, the guys who supposedly owned or were at least trying to sell her, or anyone else in New Zealand.

-Eight-
RECOVERY AND "NOT STEAL" MISSION

Steal may refer to: Theft, the illegal taking of another person's property without that person's freely-given consent

Embezzle—originally, it simply meant "steal."

How can I steal a documented U.S. Coast Guard vessel that is owned and documented by myself? The abstract of title of all owners from the day the vessel was built to the current date show the date of purchase and NO liens or encumbrances to Richard Johnson. When I returned to New Zealand to "retrieve" *Nam Sang* I carried with me the "Certificate of Documentation by United States of America, Department of Transportation, United States Coast Guard" listing the *"Owner: Richard Johnson, Sole owner—100%."*

*"Managing Owner: Richard Johnson", "Restrictions: None";
"Entitlements: None"; "Remarks: None"; "Issued at: Los
Angeles-Long Beach, CA"; Issued date: February 08, 1993".
"This certificate expires on the last day of Feb94 unless renewed
by decal on reverse."
"Signature and seal M.A. Pavloff, Documentation Officer".*

Of course officials in New Zealand would see this
differently because of the phony New Zealand registration
as well as liens and encumbrances filed against it due to the
drug runners' illegal activities.

However, according to International Maritime Law, the
only country of documentation is the country holding
title, which was the U.S. The New Zealand claims would
have to be recorded as a validated claim with the USCG
documentation office, which would then show the world
the clear owners or any encumbrances or liens on the vessel.

I was fortunate enough to know one of the most respected
maritime attorneys on the west coast. Unfortunately, his
clients were only large international steamship lines, but he
was a sailor, had a beautiful sailboat, belonged to a yacht
club, and knew of *Nam Sang*'s racing history.

My plan, if you can call it that, was to:
  • Get the "abstract of title" to make absolutely sure that
    there were no liens or encumbrances and that I had
    clear title to *Nam Sang*. This is much the same as one
    would do in doing a title search for a piece of real
    estate.

- Obtain the current USCG documentation which must be accompanied on a vessel sailing in foreign waters.
- With all of these documents I would try to make an appointment to discuss my issues.

William Vaughn was more than nice to see me the very next day. I am sure it had nothing to do with me, *Nam Sang* or making some huge hourly fee, but rather his appreciation of a fellow sailor.

My appointment was one of the most enlightening lessons I ever had. It was reminiscent of Dean Cochran in law school who could give a lecture and cover the most complex law and issues in just a few minutes. Vaughn explained my issues and situation in less than an hour and I left with a clear understanding of the law and the possibility of success in getting *Nam Sang* out of New Zealand and back under my control.

First the Law:
My papers were clearly in order. The USCG abstract of title showed absolutely no liens, claims or encumbrances of any kind. Mr. Vaughn had his own verification method, which verified the title and lack of liens.

The ship's papers (documents) were in order. Vaughn could check this with the USCG over the telephone with the Officer in Charge.

A USA documented vessel ownership, which of course included *Nam Sang*, was recognized in every civilized country in the world, and certainly New Zealand.

Secondly, the Reality:
Mr. Vaughn specifically explained his vast experience with
many similar experiences:

Not in one instance was he personally be able to retrieve
a vessel from a foreign country or actually ever know of a
maritime attorney or anyone else be able to. This is simply
because anyone and everyone imaginable will file a claim or
attachment.

My legal maritime title to the vessel would certainly be
recognized and respected, but so would all the claimants for
any and all possible obligation owed for any reason against
the vessel. For example, work done, help provided, some
injury, mooring etc, etc. Any of which will "cloud the title"
until the dispute or claim is settled.

There actually isn't enough money to satisfy all the claims,
legitimate or otherwise, to be able to get port clearance out
of New Zealand or any other country for that matter.

Legal Advice:
As a sailing friend and in the interest of not wasting your
time and money, forget your honest legal rights in New
Zealand, as it will not be successful in the long run.

Off the Record Advice:
Before I left the appointment we went into some clearly
off the record experiences in both large and small vessel
situations. Mr. Vaughn made it abundantly clear that he
in no way advises this avenue, but this has been successful

in some cases. It is extremely dangerous for many, many
reasons and went on for some time about bad results and
horrendous fatal outcomes. There were some real attention-
getting stories, discouraging in many, if not all, situations
in my case, as I knew I was dealing with some drug
related people. For some reason I couldn't express all this.
Danger, etc, didn't mean a thing to me, and even though
the marine attorney took the time to give me other stories
of their experience of self-help or a nice way of saying get
your boat out of this country any way you can and into
a United States Port where any claims can be adjudicated
with U.S. as well as international law. Not one word was
discussed about how I, or anyone else, would attempt to
get *Nam Sang*. Mr. Vaughn emphasized over and over that
he would NOT recommend this method of self-help but
also said it was the only way he had ever heard that an
owner successfully got his vessel from a foreign country in a
situation like mine.

Final and Parting Advice:
I am sure Vaughn knew what I was going to do and
mentioned the documentation numbers on the boat. I had
told him that they had been plastered over by the druggies.
He said they should NOT be removed from the main beam
because the USCG inspector will make sure himself of the
authenticity. "Wait until the USCG officer exposes the
numbers."

I must say I left Vaughn's office in somewhat a state of
shock. I had graduated from law school and was not entirely
stupid in legal issues, but what he said made sense and I

summarized the direction I would have to go, which was:

(1) Forget *Nam Sang* and the chance of ever seeing her again or

(2) Go get her one way or the other.

It took me less than one minute to easily decide what I was going to do. I was going to go get *Nam Sang* one way or the other. I was NOT in any way going to involve anyone so as to endanger them physically, legal or otherwise. I was going to get her myself and only by myself. I would love to have George along, and I am sure he would be the very first to join me, but this is going to be far more dangerous than any normal person would want to do. *Nam Sang* was mine and I could not ask a friend to take the risks for nothing more than being a loyal friend.

Now, how am I possibly going to get *Nam Sang* out of New Zealand alone?

Since 1973 *Nam Sang* was an USCG Documented vessel No. 233059 with the sole 100% owner Richard Johnson, United States Citizen. I obtained a signed copy of the Abstract of Title from the USCG Documentation Office of the original owner/builders, up to the exact current date listing all subsequent owners and all encumbrances or liens. There were *no transactions* recorded since the Richard Johnson purchase in 1973 up to and including 1993. There was no question that I had clear title to *Nam Sang* and the right to her possession in the United States of American law and under international maritime law of civilized countries in the world, including New Zealand.

What happened in New Zealand the second the Maestries
stepped off *Nam Sang* when she "arrived" in Auckland
until June 1993 would fill volumes. Their frauds,
misrepresentations, forgeries, drug smuggling, FBI, DEA's
in at least three or four countries, bankruptcies, felonies,
stealing, lawsuits, judgments, claims, arrest warrants,
jailing, deportations, to just name a few. But none of this
in New Zealand involved me! If there were any legitimate
claims against either me or on *Nam Sang* they would clearly
be shown on the abstract of title and the original USCG
document I had in my possession in New Zealand. It
couldn't be easier for any legitimate claimant to file their
claim with the USCG Documentation Office to "cloud"
my 100% ownership.

My plan was to sail *Nam Sang* out of New Zealand as
Attorney Vaughn said, before everyone could come out
of the woods and file some kind of lien on *Nam Sang* so
she could never leave the slip where she was. It could be
as simple as not getting paid for a small boat repair in the
marina or anywhere else. From what I understood, there
were hundreds of individual claimants but no governmental
agency had seized her or they would have long since taken
Nam Sang and notified the USCG Document Office the
second this boat was seized.

My Plan:
First of all I would do all my negotiations while at home
by telephone and fax, going through a yacht broker listing
Nam Sang. Meanwhile I would find out all I could about
the condition of *Nam Sang* from the latest marine survey

and who the owner or person was authorized to negotiate the sale, as well as the necessary New Zealand paperwork. As I imagined, the ownership was a mess, but I was given the name of a person who had the power to sell or maybe lease *Nam Sang*. I told him I would offer a lease purchase agreement with a final purchase price agreed upon as well as a six-month minimum lease. I faxed this guy a lease purchase agreement for one year with a first and last month payment of $2,000 a month. I immediately received a fax back with his approval to the terms. This guy could care less what we intended to do with *Nam Sang;* all he wanted was the cash, as quick as we could give it to him! Dr. Greg Howe told him a member of our Doctor group would be over within a week to bring the $4,000 US along with our signed lease purchase agreement on our behalf. There was no question that all this guy wanted was the $4,000 US NOW and the next month's payment to come as quickly as possible.

Mr. Bob Thompson, aka Richard Johnson, would fly over to New Zealand in 10 days, bringing the $4,000 cash and all kinds of marine equipment—ham radio, charts, sextant, tables, etc. that were either not available or couldn't be bought in New Zealand. The agent spent about 10 minutes on *Nam Sang,* signing the lease purchase agreement, counting the cash and some bullshit about fixing *Nam Sang* and then left as the second happiest person in New Zealand, as I was the happiest. He reminded me of a drug addict receiving some badly needed drugs (like in the movies, that is). Anyway, he was off *Nam Sang* and going to his home in some town many miles away and should be available. If there was anything I needed, to call him; otherwise, he would see me next month. Needless to say, I never saw him again.

Now I was legally, according to our lease, in possession of *Nam Sang* and with a clear understanding that we would be visiting some of the nearer islands. I showed the lease agreement to the Gulf Harbor Marina and said we would be responsible for further slip fees and I would be happy to make any payments or marina slip agreements required. They were overly nice and said they would give me their agreement in a few days, but actually never did, that I can remember. I never mentioned my name or any other name. In fact, any name I used was my own, including my car rental and credit cards, and I never used or called myself Bob Thompson. I rarely spoke to anyone, except one of the mechanics helping me with the autopilot installation and the sail maker re-stitching one of the sails. I went about working on *Nam Sang* and preparing to sail out of the marina, appearing perfectly legal and with everyone's friendly approval.

I left Gulf Harbor, Maria, Auckland, New Zealand, on a cold winter moonless night. It took no time at all to realize that although the engine ran great, the transmission was frozen up and I could not put it in gear.

Less than an hour out, a New Zealand large powerboat with at least eight non-uniformed persons came alongside and attempted to board and stop *Nam Sang*. After hours of failed attempts, unknown collision damage and increasing dangerous heavy seas and wind, they simply could not keep up, let alone board her. In these wind and seas, *Nam Sang* was comfortable and sailing at her best. She simply outran them and we were able to round Great Barrier Island and into the open sea where sea and wind conditions were building that would be fatal to a powerboat of this size. They left *Nam Sang* and me alone to attempt to survive the worst storm in these New Zealand waters in decades and make it to a United States port and jurisdiction.

The first port in this solo 38-day "escape" had to be Pago Pago, American Samoa, where the United States Coast Guard could verify the documentation and/or claims and adjudicate *Nam Sang's* rightful owner as explained by U.S. Maritime Attorney Vaughn. That was why it was so important to make an American port be the first port and not New Zealand or any other country.

Having successfully made it out of the New Zealand marina and beaten off a boarding attempt, all I had to do was sail to Pago Pago and as all mariners know, you are at sea "by the Grace of God". *Nam Sang* rounded Great Barrier Island and into thousands of miles of open seas and directly into the path of the worst wind and sea conditions I had ever experienced. In fact, I had to ask for the Grace of God.

This 38-day sail included survival of three-and-a-half days of Beaufort Scale force 12 winds and huge waves of 60 feet or more. During these three-and-a-half days the sea was completely white with foam and spray and the air was filled with driving spray and waves over the deck, which would have made it suicide to attempt going on deck.

I had learned from Thompson, the prior owner, how he
had survived a force 10 storm by centering and lashing the
wheel and letting *Nam Sang* ride out the storm with the
heading that made her comfortable.

I found that *Nam
Sang,* by some
miracle of boat
design and her
builders, did find
a way to ride
over the crest of
most of these
mountainous
waves and through the others. Not, however, without
taking on seawater to near flooding as the waves were
crashing over the deck and later through an open hatch.
Keeping the emergency bilge pump running and help from
Nam Sang and above, and a Honda generator, I kept her
from flooding.

This storm did, however, blow *Nam Sang* more than 200
miles southeast in the opposite desired course direction.
The failure of the transmission and autopilot made the
majority of the 38 days a true "sail" with an engine that ran
perfectly, but without a transmission that would engage
or an autopilot to relieve me from hands on steering. My
mental acceptance of these failures was offset by the relief of
finally getting *Nam Sang* out of New Zealand. Even being
becalmed for two days was acceptable.

Freighter in the trough of 60' waves

Nam Sang arrived safely in Pago Pago in American Samoa but not before a terrifying near disaster experience. From Fagasa Bay to Pago Pago we were only 50 feet off a lee shore with twenty-foot breaking waves and less than one knot of wind for two hours before the wind came up and we could sail away.

But it wasn't over once we harbored in Pago. *Nam Sang* was boarded by unknown foreign men and some of the same men who attempted to board *Nam Sang* when sailing out of New Zealand. They attempted to steal her but didn't know how to sail and didn't realize the transmission would not engage. Before going up on the rocks they were towed back to port and arrested for attempting to leave port without "clearing", and further deepened their guilt by presenting false ships papers to the local officials.

Gale force winds

When the USCG arrived from Honolulu, they determined three things. First, the numbers engraved on the "main beam" matched my Certificate of Documentation ("Ship's Papers"). Second, the name on Certificate of Ownership was Richard Johnson, and lastly, Richard Johnson had proper identification. The Coast Guard Officer uncovered the hidden numbers No. 233059 on the main beam and I presented an original Certificate of Documentation and my passport as proper identification. The Coast Guard Officer directed his uniformed armed assistant to escort these New Zealanders off *Nam Sang* and over to port authorities to deal with their attempt to steal this yacht. When they tried to present some New Zealand papers the officer courteously told them that he was not interested in anything they had to say or present. The adjudication of the owner of *Nam Sang* was over and even today Richard Johnson is the USCG documented owner of *Nam Sang*.

With three American crew members, two from California and one Samoan, *Nam Sang* was towed out the Pago Pago channel, but still without an auxiliary engine transmission or autopilot. We were off to Honolulu for an anticipated nice, warm sail after the first 100 miles of strong wind and forecasted heavy seas. However, now I had three crew members to share the sailing.

When safely out of the Pago Pago channel entrance and with help from one of the new crew, we raised the sails and signaled to release the tow. We were off to Honolulu in the rough and windy conditions that *Nam Sang* loved.

But where were the three crew members? Imagine my disappointment when I found all three were so seasick they couldn't move. One Californian was in the master stateroom with the door locked; the Samoan "fisherman" was in the main salon throwing up all over himself and everywhere within 10 feet and the third was lying on the cockpit seat, but at least barfing over the side.

Near exhaustion after six more hours at the wheel, and clear of the island into the open sea, I was able to arouse one crew member to hold the wheel to a compass heading in this dark night and still barf while lying on the cockpit seat. Only later I was to learn this crew member turned out to be one of the best I had ever sailed with and whom I could always count on, including what was later to happen on the sail to Honolulu.

Many of the sailors who will read this have sailed or really motor sailed through the equator's doldrums and will appreciate the difficulty of attempting this crossing without an engine. Since the invention of the engine and auxiliary power, very few sailors would attempt to sail through the equator and its dead calms without an operative engine and fuel to pass through this equatorial belt. There were times we were just sitting for days, often pointing in the wrong direction with zero wind.

Possibly the most frightening and horrifying part of this leg was going into the direct path of Fernanda, a class four hurricane and one of the worst in recorded history in the Pacific. I had ham radio contact with the Central Pacific

Hurricane Center to receive advisory bulletins from satellite and hurricane flights out of Hawaii, giving the hurricane's large "eye" path, which was itself a nightmare. This allowed us to know where to go towards the safest quadrant of the storm. Nonetheless, we tried to prepare for a possible un-survivable 145 mph wind and 80 foot seas. On August 15, 1993 it looked bad—really bad.

The excitement and fun meeting the crew's girlfriends and my wife after arriving in Honolulu was dampened by twelve uniformed and un-uniformed DEA, their dog, Immigration, Customs and harbor police searching for drugs, illegals and contraband. They searched every inch of *Nam Sang* for drugs and left a huge mess below deck without finding any drugs or apologizing for the interruption.

Then began preparation for an upwind sail through the Molokai channel around Oahu to the northern trades. Then downwind with experienced crew right under the Golden Gate Bridge under full sail, past the San Francisco Yacht Club, with everyone we knew watching. What a feeling to have *Nam Sang* home, and what an incredible accomplishment it had been!

"Aged in Saltwater" Author Bio

Richard "Dick" Williams didn't end his legendary adventures with the Pacific. He hitchhiked across the United States while chasing the love of his life, Linda, all the way to Spain. He became a well-known backcountry pilot, working the mountain airstrips of the Idaho wilderness. Taking up whitewater rafting in his

adopted, yet land-locked, home state of Idaho, he has stayed connected to life on the water.

When he's not flying or on the water, Dick is an accomplished horseman, hunter, and musician. Dick has two grown children and lives in Idaho with his wife, Linda.

"Stealing Nam Sang" Author Bio

Richard "DJ" Johnson has been a life-long sailor, pilot, and adventurer. He lived the golden age of aviation flying for various airlines around the world as well as the U.S. Air Force, and flew such classic aircraft as Constellations and L-1011s. He holds a U.S. Coast Guard Master's License and has been a blue water sailor virtually his entire life.

Made in the USA
San Bernardino, CA
22 May 2019